MY FATHER'S WAR

My Father's War

Armand Rérat

Edited by his Daughter, Gisèle Rérat

Translation from the original French by

Joyce Douglas
and
Wendy Trowbridge

First published in Great Britain in 2015 by

Bannister Publications Ltd
118 Saltergate
Chesterfield
Derbyshire S40 1NG

ISBN 978-1-909813-20-5

A catalogue record for this book is available from the British Library

Typeset in Palatino Linotype by Escritor Design, Chesterfield, Derbyshire

Printed and bound in Great Britain by SRP Ltd, Exeter, Devon

For my daughters

"L'Abnégation du Guerrier est une croix plus lourde que celle du Martyr."

Alfred de Vigny

The cover design is based on a mounted portrait of Armand Rérat, produced by the Studio J. Gerschel, in Nancy. Armand has written on the mount: "Juin 1916, en Lorraine avant notre départ pour Verdun" ['June 1916 in Lorraine before our departure for Verdun'].

INTRODUCTION

The Writing (1919)
and
Discovery of the Manuscript (2002)

M<small>Y FATHER WROTE</small> this document by hand on quarto-size paper, and apparently in one go. For many years, it lay exposed to sunlight and dust on a desk in my parents' seaside home in Vendée, until the edges of the pages were ragged. I was familiar with its appearance but not its content and I believe no one else in the family knew about it. In 1974, at my request, my father wrote a passage describing an incident in the trenches which had caught my attention. He gave me a few pages which would later become Chapter 2 of the present book, entitled 'The German Retreat From Champagne'. He also gave me a copy of 'Father Duffy's Story' published in 1919 by Father Duffy, the chaplain of his regiment, whom he had known well and admired immensely.

It was not until 2002 that I discovered the main body of the manuscript, lying at the bottom of a trunk amongst other memorabilia, in my parents' house. I did not know these seven chapters existed although I was familiar with some of the anecdotes and characters. When I found the brown envelopes I realised they contained the rest of the story of which I had one chapter. My father had spoken little of the war though no doubt he thought about it often. In notebooks full of jottings there were pages about the Americans, projects for books, and unpublished recollections.

I had already heard something of this account from my mother; for example, he had been gassed – but when? and where? Mother had spoken to me about it but without mentioning a date or a place. I was also familiar with an extract from Father Duffy's book. My father had used this in a text-book written in 1934 called 'In the English Boat' although it would seem that he himself never spoke about this dramatic event which occurred during the 'Second Battle of the Marne'. It was only in 2002, when transcribing his manuscript, that I discovered the answer to this and other enigmas. Other questions still remain unanswered: he fell from his horse and remained unconscious for several hours – where and when did that occur? And as for those few, precious photographs – what were the names of those American officers smoking cigars and posing elegantly outside the château in which they were billeted?

Father's manuscript read well, had few corrections and minimal punctuation, as if he were in a hurry to get it all down on paper and not forget anything. Eight chapters described the events chronologically, from Langres to Remagen: the Battle of the Marne (15 July 1918), the crossing of the Ourcq (July-August 1918), the battle of St. Mihiel (12 September 1918), the Argonne (October 1918), crossing Luxembourg and finally the occupation of Germany. Father later added explanatory notes here and there. The movements of the regiment and the brigade throughout the course of the great counter-offensive, which first repulsed then defeated Ludendorff's army, can be followed on the map at Page 151. The account was complete – more than complete, for the author, still delighted at the memory of his triumphal entry into Chaumont, the village near Sedan, retold this story more than once. He was the only Frenchman in the American battalion and noticeable with his sky-blue uniform. He soon became the centre of attention and the most fêted in the village.

A few words about my father, the author

Armand Rérat (1892-1976), was born at Etupes in the department of Doubs. His father was a *garde communal* and his mother did small jobs at home for the local clock makers. She kept bees and sold honey in the market. The surroundings were picturesque at that time until the development of the Peugeot industrial complex at Sochaux near Belfort at the turn of the century. My father retained a love for the countryside of his childhood, and as the fighting progressed through the north east of France in 1918, he never failed to slip into his memoirs descriptions of the plains of Champagne, the Argonne forests or the villages of the Meuse.

He went to school in Etupes and Montbéliard, then spent two years at the famous Lycée Henri IV in Paris. It was there that he acquired his love of literature and philosophy, fostered by devoted teachers such as Emile Chartier, renowned journalist, philosopher and pacifist known as 'Alain'. It is thanks to this typically French classical education that the reader will find quotations from such great writers as Montaigne, Shakespeare and Marcus Aurelius in his writing.

Once he had begun his university studies, he decided to become an English teacher and he spent a year in the English faculty at Lille University followed by a further year in London. This was no doubt one reason why in December 1917 he was called upon by the American Army to become an instructor in the 165th Infantry Regiment, 42nd Division. This was the 'Rainbow Division', with Douglas MacArthur (promoted Brigadier general in July 1918) as Chief of Staff. My father was mobilised when war broke out on August 3rd 1914. After one year's training he joined his French regiment, the 223e Régiment d'Infanterie in Lorraine. He fought at Verdun in 1916.

More training followed, this time to become an instructor, then a liaison officer with the American army. He would remain with the Rainbow Division until the end of the war, and the occupation of Remagen in Germany till the spring of 1919. It was in this year that he wrote the manuscript recounting his time with the Americans. Once demobilised, he returned to Lille to obtain the qualification which would allow him to teach students (preparing for entry into the *Grandes Ecoles)*. In 1920, he married Lucienne Vautrin, who had been a fellow student in the English department at the University of Lille.

After the war they lived in Nancy, later they moved to Sceaux on the outskirts of Paris and he taught at the Lycée Lakanal – a post he would hold until retirement. When the Second World War broke out in 1939 he was called up into the Reserve Army, and for a year we, mother and family, moved to Nantes, thought to be less dangerous than Paris. During this time, unbeknown to us, he was stationed in a town close to the Belgian border. He rejoined us after the French surrender in June 1940, and we went back to Sceaux.

He returned to teaching at the Lycée Lakanal, and also taught courses at two business schools in Paris. He retired in 1957 but continued writing. This included war memories, recollections and especially articles on English literature. He was kept busy with his family, his former pupils, his garden, and his bee-hives.

My father and the Americans

Armand Rérat was very critical of the Americans, particularly with regard to certain officers whose criminal negligence, according to him, had led to many injuries and deaths. Although he himself had undergone training with his French 23rd Infantry Regiment and had had first-hand experience of the war during three difficult years from 1915 to 1917, even he found it impossible to control independent-minded American troops who were reluctant to take instruction from a Frenchman. He retained vivid memories of those events, and his anger persisted long after. However, in 1921, when, as the newest teacher at the Lycée Poincaré, he was nominated to give an address at the prize-giving ceremony, he chose for his subject 'The Americans in France'. In his address he wrote, "We must not forget that they were fighting thousands of miles away from their homeland; they died on foreign soil, and not in defence of their own country". Over the years, gratitude had taken the place of anger.

Towards the end of World War II, after the June landings of 1944, and after the liberation of Paris on 25th August, G.I.s were everywhere in the region. A unit of Military Police was billeted at the Castel de Bellechasse in Sceaux, the town where we lived, just outside Paris, and troops in transit were camped out in the Parc de Sceaux, before moving off to chase the retreating German army. These Americans were generous, kind, plain-spoken and very popular. Here was an opportunity for the French, especially those who had experienced the First World War, and including Armand Rérat and his family, to show their gratitude and celebrate the American troops, to show them how much they were welcome, and once again to forge lasting friendships.

CHAPTER 1

Our First Battle: Baccarat
The Champagne Defensive
14 July 1918

THE REGIMENT HAD been away from the front for the last four or five weeks of training in the Baccarat sector. The generals at the headquarters of the 7th Corps, then later of the 6th, used us every day for endless practice manoeuvres in the hot June weather. Fortunately the area round Baccarat is picturesque. The countryside is beautiful. It was a pleasure for us galloping along, keeping to the edge of the woods, so as not to damage the tall grass. There were many rainy days and I remember riding in the woods when the horses got bogged down, covering the riders with mud. Colonel McCoy was a cavalryman and we enjoyed some splendid rides. Lieutenant Colonel Mitchell, who was less expert than his superior, treated us to some spectacular falls. The rest of the time, we were left to our own devices after the 7th Corps departed. However, there was always some manoeuvre in preparation, and we still did not go up to the front. We were called the 'Shock Regiment' of the Division, but we were not given any special treatment. As a major movement of the 42nd was expected, perhaps imminent, there could be no relief for any troops: this would have complicated the task at headquarters – hard enough as it was.

Waiting became interminable. During the last days we took over a battalion sector on the right and front of the Division, and occupied it for two weeks. Captain Mercier spent the first few days there, and I the next few. This was the sector of the *Rendez-vous des Chasseurs*, near Badonviller. When I went on line after a bout of the local fever, called the *dingue,* a gas attack had just taken place in Badonviller and burnt all the trees and vegetation in the ravines. I loved the outposts in these magnificent forests of fir trees. Every day I would visit the front of a company. On the right it was A Company, with Lieutenant

Martin and Captain McAddie, the Colonel's aide, and on the left, B Company with Captain Reilly, who could usually be found in his headquarters, which he seldom left. In the way of activity, our snipers would patrol the deserted positions in front of our trenches; a jumble of old networks and shelters which had been devastated by German mines. All the trees had been destroyed. One of these snipers had been killed by a German marksman. In fact these American patrols were dangerous expeditions, and we were superb targets for the Boche, whereas they kept well hidden.

We lived in a shelter below the main road from Baccarat to the Vosges which cut through the front, one kilometre further on the French side. The shelter, a splendid red sandstone building, was cut into the steep hillside. To reach it you went down two sets of steps, also made of stone, along the slopes of a small ravine. I myself lived with the interpreter in a small shelter very near the road. Naturally there were many gas alerts and we would be woken up by the mournful sound of the klaxons and sirens. They all came to nothing, but every time I had to grope my way through the wood at the rear, in complete darkness, trying to find the chicane in the networks that led to my post in the Major's shelter. This trek of 100 metres or so, sometimes took over half an hour, while I waited for the glow of a rocket before I could go on. But in this sector our comfort and peace of mind were assured.

We became concerned because a German prisoner revealed that an attack was imminent. It was to be launched against the Americans by a German shock battalion. Anxiety sometimes kept us awake at night and the men were tense, but in the daytime, what a pleasant life it was! It reminded me of the exiled princes in Shakespeare's comedies and the Forest of Arden in *As You like It*. My soul was filled with sweet melancholy among those beautiful firs with their trunks standing so straight and majestic.

Defence was very sparse in this sector: we had two companies at the front and the other two were in the rear at Neufmaisons. As a rule, the men were isolated at the end of a communication trench in groups of a few combatants: there would be a small post with a few grenadiers and a sergeant with a machine-gun. Only on the right of the front line could one move through a trench that joined the posts together. Many communication trenches spread themselves down the ravine with lookout posts, so that the forces were scattered, mostly in the front with nothing or little in reserve. Visiting the sector was very hard; you had to shuttle backwards and forwards along the trenches leading to the forward posts. There you usually found the men were vigilant, but this handful of combatants would have been totally inadequate in defending the terrain with its steep slopes and hills split by deep ravines, and the woods still unscathed by gunfire. In fact, our lines had suffered terrifying upheavals. This systematic demolition by German artillery had left us with bare first posts or even front lines exposed, whilst opposite us the Boche were beautifully concealed by a thick curtain of undamaged firs. Events in this sector of the *Chasseurs* were proof of the inadequacy of French equipment over many years and of the punishment received without being able to retaliate. They testified to our endurance and the strength of our morale, as we stood firm under raging fire in the face of such inequality, such disproportionate force and organisation.

One more word to finish with this sector: I tried hard to train the men on line, particularly by practising shooting with the VB[1]. They enjoyed setting up barrage fire in the ravine in front of them! It also built their confidence in their grenade launchers, for in the rear there had been many accidents. The American weapon had been adapted with difficulty from the French grenades launcher: they used the same grenade but the launcher, instead of being wedged in the barrel as on the French rifle, was held by means of a cartridge and this, due to a bulge in the American rifle, made the weapon much less reliable. Finally, the American bullet was a smaller calibre and did not always strike the grenade launcher, or sometimes it veered off course and struck the grenade which blew up inside the launcher. So when we were on line, I tried my best to give back the *Yanks* the confidence they had lost, and we did a few practice rounds.

At last we suddenly received the order to leave the sector. On our left were the French *Chasseurs*. The 4th American Division relieved us; we had one day's rest in Baccarat, when I met the French colonel who was to relieve us on the Ourcq. I also saw the *Chasseurs'* officer who had instructed them in America. Mercier had gone on to the brigade whilst I was attached to the Colonel. I will not describe our movements in detail, but we were certain that we were going to the Château-Thierry front, and we finally arrived in the *Champagne Pouilleuse* area in the vicinity of Châlons, after a memorable journey.

Before boarding the train I witnessed the wild indiscipline of the Americans, as they plundered a stock of wood near the line. I still remember how resentful I was every time we were billeted between Baccarat and the station, when I found out that I had been either forgotten or assigned a miserable room. But I was less hurt for myself than in my pride as a Frenchman. Having arrived at last in one of those poorly built dry mud villages, we had a well-earned rest for three or four days. How beautiful Champagne was then, with its golden wheat, its bright, vivid colours, the green valleys with their brooks lined with tall poplars, the gently undulating cultivated slopes, the contrasting fields with cereal, cornflowers and poppies of such rich hues that this chalky land seemed a paradise! At the mess we would often recite – or more usually the Colonel would recite – those particularly true lines of the Legion's poet, Alan Seegar[2] :

> *The multi-coloured flowers*
>
> *That deck the sunny chalk fields of Champagne...*

An airfield was nearby, but the battalions did not have as much time to visit it as I would have wished. Soon we went up and occupied the desert-like camps around Mourmelon. From there we could see the calm barrier of Mount Cornillet, which had been made white by shell holes. From time to time, a shell would drop on this ridge which had been French since 1917. The Americans stared in surprise at the front, so bare, so close in the clear June sky, that you thought you could touch it with your hand. Under the cloudless sky we were roasting in the camps, which had barely been used since May.

At last we received orders: we were to mount a counter-attack in the Marne area, on the east flank of the vast gap formed on our front by the German attack in May. One of our battalions would even perform a manoeuvre with tanks. I myself had to devise a practice scenario on a site the size of a pocket handkerchief. It all went wrong; the enemy groups that should have opened fire on the 3rd Battalion of the 165th Regiment had not understood their instructions and they made sure they kept out of sight, when they should have shown their presence by waving a flag! This was the signal agreed to represent a machine-gun. At any rate the tanks showed that they were able to crush the wire network, and I found out, to my great surprise, that the only way to liaise between tanks and infantry was quite simply to use the runner – the irreplace-able runner; nothing better had been invented.

But the plan for an attack was short-lived. Soon the news spread that a huge German attack on the front of the French 4th Army was imminent. This in fact was the third great offensive that we had been expecting for nearly two months. The enemy had been preparing this for a long time and in great secrecy. So, around July 2nd or 3rd we received a counter-order and departed to another camp that lay south of the second position, 7km from the Auberive front (Bois de la Lyre), on the Suippes road. It was July 4th precisely, American Independence Day, when we set up there.

I will now tell you about our first few days in this famous Châlons camp: I shall never forget that memorable night when we landed in Châlons, our long march from Châlons to Vadenay-Cuperly where we were to be billeted – a night march of course. I shall not forget that the Colonel had sent me in his car to prepare the billet at Vadenay farm, but I had the greatest difficulty finding the farm in the maze of new roads named after *Jeoffre*, after *Foch,* but not marked on the maps. Once I had found it, I could not believe that it was the farm, because the sign was cleverly concealed and the very symmetrical buildings that had always been used for training did not look remotely like a farm. After I returned to Vadenay, I was at last able to liaise by phone with the caretaker, a quartermaster and fast asleep of course: only the phone could wake him up. When I found the farm at last, I was able to send back the Colonel's car after I had wasted a whole night. To think the Colonel had asked me to send it back urgently! After all that, we were only in the farm for a very short time because the division evicted us. Unknown to us at the time, we would be returning there for a mere 48 hours, 22 days later, after the battle. Meanwhile, all this took place around June 27th or 28th. By July 4th we were destined to take part in the great defensive battle[3] which will remain such a cruel memory for me.

Anyone who has not seen the camp at Châlons in full activity has not seen anything. In 1917, when Gouraud[4] returned it was one of the best organised training centres. A clear, methodical mind had implemented excellent installations for courses on light and heavy machine-guns, aeronautics and the like. I visited the camp in 1917[5] when, as a lieutenant in the 230th French Infantry Regiment, I was sent to the course for company commanders at Somme Bionne. It was a pleasure to attend all sorts of demonstrations: the Hebert method for example, the new power of the French infantry since supplied with VBs, submachine-guns and offensive grenades. Sometimes there was a bit of bluff, of 'eyewash' in all these experiments – but I attended some marvellously accurate shooting with 37s; there better than anywhere else, I understood that the clarity of the French mind had got the upper hand over the enthusiasm and blind sacrifices of earlier years. At Châlons, they learnt how to save lives by making good use of equipment. In July 1918, the deserted camp had become a huge holding place for the reinforcements. In early July the Mourmelon civilians were evacuated; at last the attack was organised and all the preparations had been made.

At Châlons more than anywhere else, I had a strong and comforting, almost thrilling feeling that I was guided, and that a man of superior intelligence had directed our movements. For a week, I observed the continuous forward progress of our US Infantry Division and the constant, clever reinforcement of the front lines. In a first phase. we would take over all the units of two French divisions on the second position. These would then move closer to the first position, which would thus be reinforced. In my regiment, Major Anderson was made available for Commandant Nicolas, 10th and 3rd Chasseurs, at St Hilaire. In a second phase, one battalion in each American regiment would set off to reinforce the first position and thus all the French staff along the line of redoubts would become free.

For one or two days, however, we had a few problems: our limit was not clear on the right. We were assigned to the defence of Jonchery on our right (we stretched as far as the white earthworks on the left). We organised the defence of the village with Stokes and machine-guns. We strengthened the wire networks and in particular we used them to line the river Suippes, because Colonel McCoy saw this as a dangerous, easy access route if, as had been thought possible, the Boche passed the first line. In the end we were ordered to abandon Jonchery and we only occupied the second position, one kilometre to the south, as far as and including the Suippes. In the third phase the battalion which had been lent to the 1st line was moved right up to the line of resistance and would therefore contribute directly to the action.

I well remember the successful dispositions taken by the 4th Army Headquarters in defending the sector. I have just mentioned a few: the complete occupation of the second positions, 6km behind the front, in secret as far as possible. Next, the reinforcement of the first position where all the French forces freed by the Americans had pushed forward. Lastly Gouraud had conceived the astute idea of basing his defence on the following principle: to lose one or two kilometres of trenches covered by units who will signal the enemy's approach with various flares: one type for the 1st line, another for the second supporting trench, and so on. These units are sacrificed. But thanks to them the French army can use all its power to attack the advancing enemy. It will follow its movements and slow down its advance with the help of the few infantry groups of the front lines. So the German infantry is completely separated from its barrage which continues firing on its own but protects no one any more. We also know that the principle of an attack in the 1918 war was to remain behind the screen of shells from one's own artillery and overwhelm the enemy with greater numbers, using the bombardment to paralyse its machine-guns and men.

Gouraud was skilful with his defensive manoeuvres and his groups: very small in the observation trench (one squad every 500 metres for example), stronger in the support trench (half a platoon every kilometre for example), placed at the important spots of course and establishing the liaison with the French artillery. He disrupted the enemy's attack and managed to separate the German infantry from its most precious support, the artillery. In this way the Germans would arrive in front of our intermediate position (1500 to 2000m from the front line), which had in this case become the line of main resistance, strongly occupied and organised. They would then be stopped and driven back for good by this unexpectedly strong opposition.

Before telling you of the events, let me give a description of the terrain and the measures I thought were the right ones, and explain how we occupied the second and first positions.

For the first few days, from July 4th to July 9th, I spent my time organising the second line. The 3rd Battalion was on the left, the 1st on the right. We occupied the second position as said before, from the white outworks to the Suippes, therefore on a front almost 4km long, almost 5km if you followed the irregular layout of the line. We were in front of the ridge which sloped gently to the Suippes, in military terms a *glacis*, with old trench and dugouts systems, which we occupied but only sparsely. The main part of the defence was to take place on the ridge itself, much more solidly organised, and on the opposite slope. There was one reserve company per battalion: the one on the left was at the Bois de la Lyre (Fioment Ridge) in excellent shelters, the one on the right was nearer the front line (Jonchery Farm). They were camping in the open air; moreover, in spite of categorical orders, because tents could be seen from kilometres away although camouflaged. It is not easy to conceal two thousand men, especially when they are as noisy and restless as the Americans, not to mention the Service Corps and mobile kitchens. There was a continuous to-ing and fro-ing of horsemen, infantrymen, groups of reconnaissance officers, and I was astonished that the Germans were not immediately aware that the second position was occupied. It could be seen, from the balloons at least, if not directly. Fortunately the German attack was as unavoidable as destiny: the huge wheels of the enemy army had been set in motion. Everything had been planned and calculated on the other side, and no counter orders were possible.

Needless to say, the reinforcement of infantry lines was accompanied by a parallel reinforcement of the artillery. The latter extended far to the rear and had precise orders about barrages: everything had been anticipated, including the loss of the first position and a possible retreat of the artillery stationed between the first and second positions, particularly along the Suippes valley.

After I finished installing the two battalions in the second position, I went up to the lines to visit Major Anderson, in the sector of the 116th along the line of resistance, previously the intermediate position. The Americans had been ordered not to reveal their presence. Anderson had nobody at the front and the cover was French. He had been positioned between two battalions from the 116th and occupied a front of approximately one kilometre, immediately in front of the St Hilaire-Reims road (formerly a Roman road). There were two companies on the line, one with its command post at 'A' wood, almost at the Espérance crossroads, the southeast side, the other with its command post by the road. The latter was also that of the Commander of the battalion. Colonel Arnoux, commander of the 116th, was lodged in a shelter south of the road between our two companies. Finally we had H Company in reserve in miserable, 3m wide trenches. On our right, at Bois La Chapelle and Forcinal, was a battalion from the 116th, on our left at Bois Carré another battalion under Capitaine Gui. In front of us was French cover from the 3rd Battalion, Auberive 116th Regiment.

As soon as I arrived the line of resistance seemed to me quite difficult to defend. It zig-zagged through the plain of the Suippes river, which it crossed in the wood of Forcinal. It was very irregular, which was an advantage for us with regard to artillery preparation, because the Germans were not able to regulate the fire which would have revealed their batteries and intentions. But it was situated on a slight fold of the terrain and therefore above the level of the valley, so that in front of our networks there was a slight blind spot. The lie of the land in Champagne is unusually difficult for tactical purposes. If you trust appearances you might think you have a smooth plain in front of you, such as a wide river valley; it looks as though there are no undulations in the ground. But you are mistaken! Just look at that horseman galloping along over there – he suddenly disappears in a fold in the ground. Our line of resistance was excellent as far as protection from artillery went, yet bad for the field of fire immediately in front of our network. Added to this, the machine-guns were inside the network itself, and the ground in front was broken up, criss-crossed by old trenches and saps which had not been filled in – all these providing access and cover – so that it was not very favourable for machine-guns.

On arrival I ordered the following preparations, although too late for them all to be carried out. I had all the grenade launchers in each company taken to the front line. I should have mentioned that every company in the line had two levels of resistance, one beside the road and the other in a second line behind them, so that two platoons in each company were in the front trench and the other two were in support. The machine gun companies were distributed according to the terrain, with one or two platoons on the front line and the rest between the front and second line or on the second line itself, so that several could strafe the road. It seemed to me that the *VB*, an excellent grenade launcher with a 150m range, was the perfect weapon on this terrain where you could advance without being an obvious target to machine guns or infantry rifles. Finally I drew the Americans' and Colonel Arnoux's attention to the necessity of keeping a very close watch on those wide communication trenches coming down from the evacuated front to our present line. They were two or three metres wide, worn down by shelling and furrowed by rain; they could be used for an advance under cover from machine-guns and almost four abreast. I am not exaggerating.

I had been right in thinking that the Boche would advance using the saps and old trenches and would not expose themselves as a target unnecessarily. In fact, defence became the job of the artillery, VB grenades, Stokes[6] and hand grenades. Unfortunately, I did not have time to have the Stokes brought in before the attack. They arrived on the 15th, in the middle of the day, after the Boche had already struck. But I reinforced the VBs in the front line. I had munitions taken there, VB grenades mostly. I had more barbed wire network prepared to block up the old trenches which were gaping cracks.

I explained the tactical situation to the two captains and the officers in the line, showed them the dangers of the terrain that had been ploughed up and the small blind spot outside their networks. More than that: I visited Colonel Arnoux on July 14th, somewhat late, and drew his attention to the inadequacy of the obstacles set up to close the trenches in front of the line of resistance and the fall-back line. Strangely, nobody could see the danger! Under the Roman road, which was roughly parallel to our front and merging with our support line, there were trenches which could have saved the enemy crossing over the road, and saved them from the relentless battering of our machine-guns! But there was nothing to block the passages underneath, not even provision for a single grenadier to guard them. It is by his foresight and attention to details as vitally important as these that you recognise a leader. Colonel Arnoux claimed that there was already enough barbed wire every-where along the front of his regiment to fill all the trenches in the world – even so, he conceded that his pioneers would get to work on this and that my Americans would receive the shells, VBs and wire rolls that were needed.

I went up in the line too late and of course all this did not occur to me on the first day. How could it have? Assessing such a situation as this requires some reflection. First, I needed about two days to get to know the terrain, trenches, machine-gun locations. It was only then, around the 12th or 13th, that I could form an opinion and defend it vigorously, either against the Americans or the French. It is strange to reflect how few are the people who think, either in life or in action, and how little they think. I was not in the regular army[7]. I was not even concerned directly in defending the front line. My place was with my Colonel, 7km away, in a trench 8 metres deep! Yet after two days I had much clearer and firmer ideas about what the German attack would be like, not only better than my American major – this would be quite natural – but even better than the French colonel who had been in the sector for weeks.

I have often found in a battle that even the bravest men are not the most sensible, and that courage is often accompanied by stupidity; or to express it better, courage and sangfroid are completely different things. I have seen a number of brave men lose their heads, and while I did not particularly distinguish myself by my gallantry, I found to my satisfaction that I was able to anticipate and to act in situations when officers with more guts were not. I have always been appalled by the distressing attitude which made people prefer courage to sangfroid in a regiment, and mix up these two qualities, different though they are. Here is an example: at Reillon, in October 1915, I saw my entire company crammed in the trenches, stupefied, stunned, because they had just been through a teargas barrage, and not a single officer would give them an instruction. Meanwhile the Boche were attacking one of our trenches under our noses, but no one would shoot because no one had given the order! Furthermore, a regular army officer in my company refused to obey me when I gave the order to shoot because the captain himself had not given the order! Such is the absurdity of discipline when it is not moderated by common sense, and courage when it is not combined with sangfroid.

I am not exaggerating when I say that I quarrelled with everybody about these wide trenches. I wanted to block them at the first sign of a German invasion but was always met with objections. *'Only if the French retreat…'* or *'The danger is not so great.'* We tend to assume that the enemy will commit the same blunders as ourselves. Admittedly, the French might have launched an attack using the embankment, although no experienced infantrymen would have done so. But as for the Boche, I knew they would keep out of sight, advancing under cover.

Those July days will remain in my mind forever. They are the quintessence of my war memories. I was totally absorbed in the sense of responsibility that keeps a leader going. And I was proud to be responsible for these 1000 Americans in such an important sector. How beautiful this month of July was, and how calm! The Germans suffered all our bombardments without a murmur. They had obviously decided that an ominous silence would be the rule all along the front. Were they hoping to intimidate us and make us nervous with this unnatural lack of activity? Would they keep their secret even better and conceal the front and their feverish preparations by maintaining complete silence? But we knew all about the danger facing us. Every day Gouraud's army took prisoners in several places and seldom did a day go by without the front being lit up by multiple flashes from a distant, soundless bombardment. Innumerable German and French rockets would soar into the sky and then drop slowly, their red and green signals of two or more stars glimmering in the distance, forming an extraordinary spectacle.

Anyone who has not listened to the faint rumble of a distant battle or witnessed, even as a spectator, the glow of the artillery and the brief reddish flashes of the percussion and time shells, cannot imagine the huge sadness such a sight aroused in me and the depth of my reflections on human nature and life. How lonely one felt during these beautiful nights, facing possible, perhaps imminent death. How insignificant life felt, a spectacle as transient and petty as the mean and murderous battle out there! All around, in the distance, parts of the sky would be lit up by the mournful signalling of the French or the Germans, each in their own language expressing their emotions, betraying alarm, anxiety or pain. Some were desperate messages to the artillery, to their companions or to the rear; others expressed the nervousness or unease of some isolated sentry. And all along that twinkling line of fleeting, multi-coloured lights, all along the barrage of fireworks which barely rose above the distant horizon, along the zig-zagging, undulating line of red, green and white flames which marked the front, men were suffering and asking themselves why they were there. Yet they stayed and went on killing each other, not knowing what it was all about, not feeling hatred for their enemy. They had no feelings other than the sadness of dying and suffering, and the vague longing for another life and another less demented universe.

Every night the probes kept us informed about the enemy's preparations. Planes would send us the positions of the new batteries, and on land our observation post would let us know of any daytime movements. From July 10th onwards, the attack seemed imminent. Lookout posts noticed dense traffic in spite of the Germans' precautions. We heard that officers had been seen reconnoitring at the front (their attacking troops never went into the sector until the day before or the night of their attack). Finally, for several successive nights (July 12th–14th) we even started our artillery barrage because of false alarms. We took our first dispositions. Our reserve company (Pontier) working every night on behalf of the French (Capitaine Firin) levelled the maze of abandoned trenches in front of the line of resistance, since this could have given the Germans such good cover. At last July 14th arrived without the slightest incident, and the Boche hardly condescending to shoot a single shell. To the end, this dead calm kept us in doubt and uncertainty, hoping that nothing might happen and there was no real danger. While taking the last dispositions we did not fail to make fun, as was to be expected, of the orders of such a timid commander and to keep pretending we were not anxious in spite of it all.

A memorable day, July 14th. Colonel McCoy was to collect me during the day in his car. I had not gone in line to stay there; my place was with the Colonel as soon as Anderson was settled, and this was nearly done. Just about everybody had understood their mission and every situation had been prepared for. As usual we had lunch with Captain Kelly. Round the table were Major Anderson, so young, happy and healthy; McDermott, his assistant and Lieutenant Smith, in charge of food supplies, the young officer that would lose his life the next day; and finally Father Duffy of whom I intend to write a portrait in due course. About 1p.m. I decided to go round the sector once more, as the Colonel had phoned to say he would collect me around 3p.m. in his car because he wanted me to spend the 14th July celebrations with him. But going round the sector took longer than I thought. In a number of places, I was

16

stopped by the officers and even the men. The machine-gun people showed me round their positions. Then when I came back to Colonel Arnoux's command post (PC Jerome) I had a further wait before communicating some of my remarks to the French colonel, who had not finished talking to the colonel commanding the brigade. So that when I finally arrived at Major Anderson's command post I discovered that Colonel McCoy had not waited for me. I am glad about this now because I would have missed the most beautiful spectacle of the war and I would not have taken part in it.

They served us dinner early. Two French officers were invited in return for services rendered to the battalion through their knowledge of English. Only one could come, De Courcy. We drank and sang blissfully. The French regiment even taught the Americans an American song.

The prettiest girl I ever saw / Was sucking champagne through a straw.

That evening our corrugated iron shelter was the scene of a very lively dinner to celebrate the 14th of July. After dinner we all dispersed, as it was getting dark. Then, as we sensed the coming storm, Father Duffy (*the Roman Catholic Chaplain of the Irish American Infantry Regiment*) and I went round the trenches nearby, and I witnessed Roman Catholic ceremonies that were moving and grandiose in their simplicity.

Francis Duffy still represents in my eyes the ideal American citizen. Like perhaps the greatest number of Americans he was of foreign origin and was very much the Irish type in sentiments and turn of mind: he was an Irish patriot as well as an American. Above his great American country, or alongside it, he placed Ireland – his own small, oppressed country. However, he had nothing to do with Sinn Fein. I believe he accepted the Irish resistance to English influence as the inevitable attitude of any self-respecting Irishman. Deep down he submitted to, rather than lent himself to the dislike his regiment felt for England, and to this he owed his ability to influence the men. He was a demigod for the regiment. His qualities have become legendary, for he cut a fine figure in action, as early as in the battle of Champagne when he went and fetched the wounded and buried the dead. Later, on the Ourcq, the cruellest task fell to him, bringing moral support to hundreds of wounded men in a first-aid post in the middle of a bombardment battering Villers-sur-Fère. Under the shells which rained down on the village and hastened the end of the dying in the school, right in the centre of the German shelling, with a smile on his face he handed out cigarettes to the wounded being carried away. To others he gave absolution with a few supremely comforting words. Father Duffy knew each man in the regiment by his first name and surname; to some he had taught the catechism and they took their first communion with him. Together with the ability to store every fact in his memory he had a deep sense of human philosophy and knew how he must make his influence felt, where and when necessary. I have seen him slap the face of a drunken man without anger, as a father would punish his child. He was the father of this whole regiment, the soul of this crowd. He personified the best of Ireland, and the men sensed this; he combined a brilliant mind and a noble character, and most of all the wisdom and experience drawn from meeting and observing thousands of men from all walks of life.

Father Duffy had immense knowledge. He had taught philosophy in a seminary. His church was one of the wealthiest and most prosperous in New York, and he always had vast sums of money available, which the Irish Americans had sent him. He had a tough childhood, went to work at the age of twelve, did all sorts of manual jobs. And now he had become the personification of all that was good for these 3000 Irishmen. He knew how to speak to them, and no other proof of his deep wisdom is needed than the success he achieved without looking for it in action. On the evening of 14th July, I accompanied him on his clergyman's round. He had a premonition that it would be the night of the battle, and as we walked through the trenches, after exchanging a few words with 'the boys' about their families, he would simply say in a thoughtful voice, 'Let those of you who wish to, pray and ask forgiveness for your sins, and I shall give you absolution.' In the July night with its sky still light and the stars still faint, these rough, unrefined Americans would meditate for a moment, and Father Duffy forgave them their sins with a great sign of the cross. There was nothing more to say, and we would move to the next group.

I am sure that this memory is one of the most beautiful among those Father Duffy took back with him from the war. He had sensed danger, he had prepared these men's souls to the idea of the supreme sacrifice when the battle was only a few hours away. So much foresight and human wisdom – wisdom in action – are qualities not often found, and to my knowledge not so happily combined. Father Duffy's independent approach to religious ceremonies would have shocked a French priest. On the eve of a battle he would give communion to good Catholics without hearing their confession, simply asking them to repent. What do you expect? It was impossible to hear three or four hundred confessions, and these men were going to their deaths.

I myself have moving memories of Father Duffy. With his last visit on the day before that battle, he contributed more to the Americans' determination than all my pathetic predictions and all the preparations of the French and American commands. The noble gesture of the chaplain giving absolution to these bending, helmeted men with their tough profiles, is one of the most moving images of the war in my memory. What power there was in this man who, with his hand upraised, inspired remorse in those unpolished souls! And immediately they were consumed with overwhelming gratitude for God's generous forgiveness. Even if there were no life after death, these men were really born again to a new life at that instant. They disowned their past and became souls inspired by generous resolve and the will to die or to conquer. Who could count the times that Father Duffy, giving unsparingly of himself to men dying on the battlefield, brought the solace of his friendship, his sympathy, his smile, the comfort of his example and of his unassuming courage?

That evening the interpreter had gone with the Firin Company and took them to work as usual to translate the French officer's instructions to them. Old trenches had to be levelled. It was dead calm in these lines – on both sides, only the silence of the night, the unchanging sky, motionless above the mutilated Champagne country. Anyone who has been in a war will have savoured that moment of calm before the storm when one views life with extraordinary detachment, like an impartial spectator getting ready to leave it. Like Montaigne's philosopher, such men had spent long years preparing themselves for Death as a natural event. They waited their turn, and Death would always come and take them one by one. Animal fear drove soldiers to lie low and hide from the blows, but at the same time they felt the melancholy, yet superb detachment, of those who are seeing the world one last time, preparing themselves to leave it. I cannot think of any books to describe a soldier's soul better than Meditations by Marcus Aurelius, the noble-hearted soldier-emperor.

About 11pm, I went back to the battalion command post. A moment later, the latest information arrived: the attack was certain. It was a quarter to twelve. One of our reconnaissances in a neighbouring regiment had brought back four prisoners from the attacking troops. The shelling was to start in a quarter of an hour, about midnight, and the infantry attack would be launched about

4a.m. At the command post, we were in turmoil, our hearts wrung by emotion: this could be our last night. We dispatched runners to warn the companies, but they did not have time to get to the company command posts before the German bombardment started. To pre-empt this, our artillery had opened a running fire on the enemy trenches and batteries. On our side, the sky was aglow with all the lights of this booming artillery, whose projectiles were swishing high above our heads. This fire, ahead of enemy fire, brought us joy and comfort. At the command post we felt uneasy under our arched iron roof and our few sandbags. Moreover our shelter was completely open at the front, without the slightest protection: putting up a wall had been one of my plans but had not been brought to fruition. Without doubt one single shell on the trench would kill us all, but the lazy Americans never got round to building the wall!

Suddenly, around midnight, the first shell dropped, and the shower of missiles started. In our area, some 50m behind us, the road was hit the most, by percussion and time shells, 105s and 150s. The batteries at the rear were probably hit quite a bit too. Our shelter was spared during the initial assault, as the Germans bombarded the road or scattered their missiles haphazardly. The horizon was lit up on each side, but this time the German artillery was unquestionably superior. Soon acrid gas fumes got in our throats; we started sneezing and had to put on our masks. At the command post there was nothing left for us to do for the moment; we would just have to fight for our lives if the Germans managed to cross the first lines. I deeply regretted having left my revolver at McCoy's headquarters, but fortunately there were grenades all around to be used. I sat on one of the bunks, Father Duffy in a corner on another; the Major sat on a chair at the table. We waited with anguish in our hearts and looked at each other in dismay.

Fortunately, there was good news: Captain Kelly came to tell us about his company who were not suffering too much from the bombardment. In the end we had few dead or wounded during these three or four hours of preparation. It was the barrage, sweeping the terrain systematically, that caused the most casualties. About 4p.m. this inferno was still booming around us. Our artillery seemed completely silenced: only a few flashes lit the sky on our side. We were alive. But how was it going in the front line? We were completely cut off from the rest of the world, without news and all we could see was happening immediately around us.

About half past four came the hardest moment. For a short time – a few minutes – we thought we were done for; 150s rained on overhead and blew out our candle. A shell dropped on the parapet of the trench outside the door, blasted the major off his chair and injured my knee slightly. A moment later two more shells dropped in the trench, killing and wounding liaison men. We were stunned. We thought our time had come. Only later, when calm followed this storm of fire, did I understand we had just been under the barrage from the Boche artillery. We got out of our shelter. Soon, some 500 metres away, a German machine-gun opened fire from the heights on the other side of the Suippes river. Then others started their rat-a-tat. The front lines had long since sent their barrage rockets and our artillery was going all out. Captain Graff, from the machine-guns, thought he could recognise his own from their whistling sound! After an impassioned discussion we made our battle preparations around the command post. We sent the yellow flare – *the enemy has reached the line of resistance* – and our 75s grazed over our heads. It was getting light, a clear July morning, and the first German planes appeared, flying very low and looking for their infantrymen who had stopped in front of our first positions.

From then on we received news from the French in the front lines and from Firin, the company in reserve. Colonel Arnoux asked for half the Firin Company to counter attack on the Suippes where it seemed we had lost two positions. Captain Kelly was also asking for reinforcements and we grudgingly sent the few men we had left with Firin; these men had been caught ahead of the line of resistance by the German barrage, and, under enemy preparatory fire, they had rejoined their alarm posts leaving a great number of dead and missing. As responsible officers we only sent as many as we could afford when we assessed the requests for reinforcements, taking into account the stress caused by the battle. We sent a lot of ammunition and large numbers of VBs but very few men. A few hours later, the thunder of the barrage was still rumbling on through hills and plains towards Châlons, along the Suippes valley and over our rear; we did not get a single shell. Soon however, German aircraft came and fired at us with their machine guns, swirling above us like dangerous birds; soon their trench shells dropped on our front lines some 50m from us, and did a lot of harm as they raked the trenches we occupied and caused many casualties.

Thus, that day we lost quite a few men and one officer, Young, who I thought was so brave, so staunch and enthusiastic when in the early morning he went up to take command of a platoon whose leader was wounded. In a corner of our first line, American corpses piled up under the onslaught of German grenades and trench shells. The Germans got very near by using the small fold in the terrain which I have mentioned, and one of our machine-gun sections was destroyed by grenades thrown through its barbed wire protection.

The Germans had stopped, for sure. They were just in front of our lines and occupying old trenches south of Auberive. The Americans claim that as they fell back they were assailed by bullets shot by their own troops to stop them withdrawing, but I rather think that their comrades were actually protecting their withdrawal. The roads behind Auberive on the small chalky hills were cluttered by artillery convoys. We did not know what to expect: tanks, cavalry? But in fact the accompanying German batteries had followed the movements of the infantry and were taking position in the open fields behind the occasional hedge, barely 2000m from our trenches, and opening fire on us from this distance. Unfortunately our artillery, which had been busy all night, had long since become silent. Our artillerymen were exhausted and taking a rest. So the German deployment of forces was not as deadly for them as it might have been.

The worst was over. The rest of the day was spent peacefully gathering the innumerable anecdotes of the battle. A memorable one was Father Duffy's. As he was walking around the trenches to look after the wounded, he saw a French Poilu slipping away along a trench, holding under his arm a bottle of champagne from 14 July celebrations. A time-shell came: the man clamped himself against the parapet. But he would have done anything, said the good Father, rather than let go of his bottle.

We evacuated our wounded, quite a number of them and becoming even more numerous, because the dense American lines had suffered much more than the French under the direct, rapid fire of the Germans. In addition I feel certain that the Americans made themselves conspicuous with reckless, unnecessary movements which gave away their presence to the German aircraft: they were unaware of the danger. Thus, in two days' fighting we lost nearly 200 men, while the French battalion on our left only lost 20, the one on our right, along the Suippes, 70, and the covering battalion about 100 because many of its men had been taken prisoners.

The Americans said they had scarcely seen a dozen Germans. This does not surprise me: even accounting for the observers' wildest imagination, the figures in the enemy lines only ranged from 20 to 50. To put it another way, the Germans gave nothing away. At our command post we could only see the horizon above Auberive by climbing on the top of the shelter, and for the area out to100m in front of us we had to rely on other people's reports. The machine-gun company worked wonders. Every time their machines got jammed by a shell the Americans took them to the company command post where they would be cleaned and put right again. In this way the machine-gun sections were kept going by reinforcements sent by the support line. On our left, F Company had not suffered much, apart from the captain, who was nearly buried in his shelter by a 150 shell which burst through the roof.

I was so tired on July 15th that my memories of the day are blurred. Hours went by, gloomy and dismal; I hardly noticed. I know that I dreaded the planes. We stayed in the command post although we should have visited the line. I was too tired to take the initiative. I did not mention the following incident before: on the night of 14th-15th July, about 5a.m., a liaison agent came in, with his hand torn off, followed by another soldier, to take refuge under our arched roof. The major first let them stay, then changed his mind and with typically American – and soldier-like – harshness, he threw out these disabled men who were in our way and distressing us with their moans. This was cruel but fair: pity has no place in a battle.

On the 15th, the Germans made another attempt, but without confidence or enthusiasm. The attack we had stopped on the first day started again, with the shelling and the planes and so on, but half-heartedly this time. On the morning of the 16th, our first position was under attack again between 9a.m. and midday. This time we maintained excellent liaison. The Colonel, having kept his telephone line, transmitted our information, and we asked for the barrage to be directed in front of our threatened headquarters. It was a delight to hear our 75s whizzing towards the enemy as they were trying to advance using the trenches. Sometimes they had to be chased with grenades. On the 17th, a French unit commander on our right told me that some Americans on his left, agitated and perplexed because a few Germans had entered their front line, had asked him for advice. His sergeant had to go over to the Americans and show them what they had known so well before the battle and had simply forgotten, i.e. how you advance with grenades and bayonets, and how you mop up a position. But there were no leaders left in the units because Kelly had lost all his officers, either wounded or killed. The Americans, not trained to take the initiative, and having no skill in manoeuvring, held their ground only by virtue of numbers and sacrifices.

I still remember the painful night of 15th-16th, the failures of all our efforts during those two days. Only on the 16th, after the last German attack and when our command post was moved to Jerôme, did we get a bit of warm food. In fact, about midday on the 16th, after the second failed German attack, we heard through our couriers that the French colonel was nowhere to be found. So there was no leader left, but the Engineers' lieutenant only let us know this about 3p.m., which was rather late. All in all, for this commander to withdraw without warning his people gave a bad impression, even though he had been ordered to do so. Be that as it may, *we were the front line now*. Straight away I decided to go and occupy Command Post Arnoux, which was more secure and spacious and, moreover, in the centre of the battalion. We travelled over a terrain that was strewn with branches from the roadside trees, yet although changed, was not too disturbed, and we set ourselves up in Command Post Jerôme, where we had an underground telephone link with the Colonel.

That battle was over. Normal life was resumed. Immediately the French asked us to propose names for a Legion of Honour award, two military medals, and also some Military Crosses. The Americans were never awarded the promised decorations, yet they had been counting on them, and often mentioned this to me in the last months of the war . Colonel McCoy sent Lieutenant Colonel Mitchell up to the lines. Mitchell became commander of the American troops in the sector after the lines had been further reinforced with the 2nd Battalion of my American regiment; this was on the morning of the 16th, at the very moment when shelling announced the second German attack. This 2nd Battalion was the one I had instructed, with Major McKenna, Cane, Meaney, Hurley, Ryan, and Merle-Smith.

Mitchell settled down in our command post and, good regular soldier that he was, refrained from concerning himself with any of the important questions. In this case however, it was a wise decision, as we knew the sector better than he did. Moreover, the 3rd Battalion was not under our command but led by Captain Gui. Our troubles were over. The 17th went without incident, except for the torture I suffered spending the night on a chair whilst all the liaison people occupied the bunks. American leaders do not sleep! Anderson spent the night sitting on a chair and dozing next to Mitchell, on the pretext of working. Only Mitchell eventually went to bed. As for myself, I could not stand it any longer; I found a bunk and slept for a few hours, until I was brought back to life and given the job of translating the French colonel's orders. Strangely, headquarters staff seem unable to understand that their subordinates need to rest. Never overworked, they keep a calm mind – less so perhaps at times of action, but still calm because there is less immediate danger for them. They judge others by their own feelings, and therefore lack the imagination which is so essential to a leader. Paper work, so-called *urgent* reports, descend on you at times when you could be sleeping.

All I have to relate now is our very unexpected relief. On the 17th we had a visit from the head of the French Mission accompanied by the chief of staff of the 42nd US Infantry Division, Colonel MacArthur. He was a likeable man if ever there was one, with a handsome youthful face, lit up by a fine smile. During the war MacArthur was to the 42nd Division what Duffy was to the regiment. He organised the Division, formed it as a unit, an army able to fight. In the rear he put to use his experience with his work, his enlightened mind, his trust in French military skills; and in the front line, his courage and his boldness were matched by his good fortune. On the evening of the 17th, news of our relief came unexpectedly, after Gouraud had given orders to attack to regain the lost ground. On the 17th, I went down to Command Post McCoy to have a wash, a rest and a change of clothes. I went down from the lines in the headquarters Commander's luxurious car and went back up the next morning after a good night's rest. On the road from St Hilaire to Jonchery I noticed the ravages caused by the German artillery – the road strewn with the corpses of horses already swollen, and field kitchens blown up just as they were moving. Finally, Colonel McCoy came to visit us on the 18th and went round the front line trench, where they informed him of the suspicious behaviour of a French officer. I was that officer. In fact I had been mistaken for a spy because the 2nd Battalion did not know me. On the evening of the 19th the relief order suddenly came around midnight. Our raids had shown that the Germans were withdrawing their shock divisions; we, on the other hand, had launched our Chateau-Thierry offensive.

Colonel Arnoux had gone to bed and did not get up to write a relief order himself. It was better this way, for the French majors arrived at Command Post Jerôme, coughing and spluttering as if they were at death's door: the enemy were shelling with teargas to conceal their retreat. We worked out the relief orders, most complicated because we were being relieved by men from two different battalions, and also men from different companies of these two battalions relieved each of ours. In the end this relief did not take place, because the Americans left the sector as soon as they saw the first Frenchmen in their trenches. The takeover was very slow. Our last units left in broad daylight. I served as an interpreter, as a guide, whatever. We were free. I left with Mitchell and tried to use the Mourmelon road, but I lost my way, and in the end I decided it would be preferable to go via St Hilaire and Jonchery, which is what we did. The regiment came back from the lines in utter disorder (mostly the 2nd Battalion), so this provoked angry scenes from the Colonel. On the evening we left, the situation promised to become quite bearable at Command Post Jerôme: we received a parcel of fruit, wine and cheeses from Command Post McCoy. We left it for the people behind us, having first stuffed ourselves.

This was a prosaic ending to the great battle of Champagne, which was so momentous in the history of the war and the turning point of the year 1918. I had met a brave, good soldier, Anderson. I had won McCoy's and Mitchell's esteem. So much for me. We thought we were going down to get a rest. A burden was lifted from our minds once we left those white trenches of Champagne and once we had buried our poor dead. The men had suffered a lot. While those in the front lines had done their duty, the others, cooks, fatigue parties, had all fled, abandoning the field kitchens. The front line was practically without any food supplies for at least two days; only at the end did these important services begin to function normally. I wrote at length to Colonel Corbabon, reporting on the causes of American losses as well as the failings in liaison – for which the Americans were not always responsible – and the complete absence of food during the battle. I felt happy and light-hearted as I came back from the front: I had a clear conscience. But how exhausting this laborious march was on the dusty roads! In the rear, I was told that the shelling had seemed fearful from a distance, but on the second position the losses were light. It appears we had become seasoned fighters at little cost. We were billeted in Vadenay that day.

Finis Champagnae

CHAPTER 2

The German Retreat in Champagne:
July-August 1918

IT IS ONLY a few months since these events took place, but they already seem so far away, so unreal – one soon becomes re-accustomed to comfort. There was a time when I would lie down with delight and feel wonderfully refreshed if I so much as had a bed to sleep in. We were billeted in Vadenay one day. I had time to send Colonel Arnoux the list of men to be mentioned in dispatches. I remember the argument I had with Sidleman the next day, 21 July, at Vadenay-Village. The men had arrived very tired, and as the billeting officer had not been quick enough in making the premises available – his lordship did not like being disturbed at night – they had broken into the barns and used the material as the fancy took them. I remonstrated angrily about this to the Lieutenant Colonel's aide, Sidleman, and to the Colonel a few hours later. When I remarked to Sidleman that French soldiers would never have behaved in such an unruly manner, he declared angrily, 'Of course! They have no guts. They wouldn't dare!' The notion of discipline was so undeveloped in this officer that he mistook it for weakness of character.

Throughout their time in France the Americans found it difficult to accept being employed as officers' orderlies. They were willing in principle, but they were rather clever in evading all the compulsory duties. On many occasions I had American orderlies, but that was only on paper; for I could never get so much as even a pair of shoes polished, except later, when I had a well-disciplined Greek soldier who had been in the Foreign Legion.

That same evening we got on the train under attack from German bombs. A huge battle was raging in Château-Thierry which seemed to be going well for us. That is where we were heading .We boarded the train and on 22 July we arrived at La Ferté-sous-Jouarre, on the Marne river. The railway station had been completely destroyed by air strikes. That same night we were billeted in a luxurious chateau in a village by the Marne,. As usual, McKenna, the Colonel's aide, with his spiteful ways, had arranged for me to sleep in an attic room. I preferred to sleep comfortably on my own in an outbuilding. At that point I was annoyed and angry with the Colonel, as not only had he not taken me to Gouraud's debriefing of the battle, under the artificial pretext that only high-ranking officers were invited; but moreover, as Gouraud had invited him to dinner, McCoy instructed his orderly, Lieutenant Preston, to go with him instead of me. Preston was the son of the Deputy Director of the Red Cross in Paris, a pleasant young man whom I felt sorry for.

The Americans, most of all the Irish or Scottish Americans, are cliquish. The regiment was practically divided into castes: the Irish and the non-Irish. The real Irish, who were entitled to the shamrock, would sit round the Colonel, or the company commander in each company. They would get praise and promotion. Furthermore McCoy, although an enthusiastic soldier and a charming man, was ambitious and concerned about his promotion. He believed it was not a good thing, it was even humiliating, that he should be accompanied by me, his assistant officer, an unimportant French infantry lieutenant, when he was to face a great man like Gouraud. He wanted to meet our great leader on equal terms.

So many arguments I had with those Americans! Or rather so many insults to our uniform that I have had to put up with! This was quite usual: Mercier was faced with the same problems at the Brigade Headquarters. In combat the Americans knew where to find me, but they preferred to do without me, unless my advice turned out to be excellent, in which case they were willing to make use of my ideas another time.

Here, I must write a few words about Colonel McCoy, as he became the dominant figure during the next few days. A well-mannered man, he was of medium build and brisk, with a face tanned from the sun of the Philippines. A bachelor, he was always dressed with elegance to the point of fussiness, and his immaculate white shirts were a matter of pride to him. Moreover, he was an excellent rider. He came from the Chaumont Headquarters[8], as did our French commanders. I believe he was a volunteer. He was a kind-hearted man, although he could sometimes appear rather superficial and over-enthusiastic. His Army experience was interesting: once he had taken part, as a lieutenant, in an American military mission observing German manoeuvres, and had got to know the Kaiser, having dined at his table. In the US, he had been Theodore Roosevelt's aide-de-camp and was one of his warmest supporters. He would often speak of Roosevelt's family, whom he knew intimately. He was a conversationalist and liked the good things in life, always bringing quality guests from Chaumont or Paris; and he brought liveliness and interest to the otherwise dull mess at the regiment's headquarters. He was easily carried away, quick-tempered, sharp but very pleasant company, courteous and a great admirer of the French, particularly those of Chaumont! He often had original ideas: in Baccarat, he had thought of setting up a band long before the American Headquarters had ordered it; he arranged for the purchase of bugles and other instruments. He took an interest in getting his officers educated and had asked me to buy about fifty good French history books, novels and memoirs. He was not a hard worker, nor always very effective, since he did not recognise the necessity or value of clear, coherent and methodical thinking; in war, he relied on the inspiration of the moment and his undoubted drive. McCoy was not an officer à la française.

The next day, or the day after, from La Ferté-sous-Jouarre I went to Paris with Father Duffy. McKenna, the Colonel's aide, and Captain Morgan of the Supply Company, had already set off the day before. They did not reappear for a week. I, on the other hand, spent a rather grim day in Paris and returned to our billet the same night. There an order was awaiting us: to set off in lorries to the region of Chateau-Thierry(?). I had been well advised to return so soon. On the 24th, the whole day was spent trying to find out which lorries were to take us, since the orders were so vague. Finally, after visiting the various battalions and not getting any lunch, we found the Regiment had assembled at the boarding place. The lorries arrived at last, but there were long arguments. Major Donovan wanted to do as he pleased and refused to take any orders from a mere lieutenant in charge of transport. We had to explain that he should leave it to the person in charge and that all this had nothing to do with him. Incidentally, the officer in question that day was a brute of a colonial regiment who had been put in command of the coloured drivers.

We got off at Epieds in broad daylight, amid clouds of dust and in full view of the German planes waiting for us. I was worried that so many men were concentrated in one place and afraid that the enemy would attack us. Epieds was well within reach of their guns, since even in Trugny, further back, the Germans had been firing shells that same day. We billeted in the woods near the village, the Colonel and I in the chateau, joining the general in command of the French Infantry Division. We were surrounded by German batteries of 155s. The general was stationed where a German general had been, only a day earlier. When I say the *chateau*, I mean an outbuilding next to the chateau. The only beds we had were the floor, a marble billiard table, and the loft, which had straw left by the Germans. I must say I much preferred the billiard table. The French invited us to dinner, but they did nothing to give us decent accommodation, and our Colonel slept on a chair. I lay down on the billiard table, covered with my greatcoat, and I have never been so cold, nor slept on such a hard bed as on that table. That was on the 25th.

That day brought nothing but orders and counter-orders – and disorder. The French did not know what they wanted. The major-general only wanted his division to be relieved, but the High Command sent him the order to advance and go into the attack. One of our battalions even set off on the evening of the 25th, laboriously assembled in the middle of the night in the woods where they were camping, under orders to show no light. After they had walked a few kilometres, the absurd order was countermanded: no reconnaissance had been made. I remember extreme confusion in the plans of the French command, and the American orders on top of the French ones made my task even more difficult. All these people were confused or tired. According to the major-general who wanted to be relieved, the French units were bewildered, exhausted and much reduced in numbers: indeed I noticed this. I still remember an order to relieve the French on the 25th, which came so suddenly that all the captains were missing because they had gone to reconnoitre the positions. So great was their haste that the 1st Battalion, whose turn it was to go to the front line, set off without a captain or the major. All this because a general couldn't wait to be on the move. But after all, he was only thinking of his exhausted and overtaxed men.

Thus on the 24th I had seen Paris again and on the 25th I slept on a billiard table, a hundred yards away from two long-range 155s! Such is a soldier's fate. One day it is life and all its pleasures; a few hours later it is the battle, bloody, fierce, the battle for survival, the supreme effort to save your skin and your honour at the same time. What days those were! I remember departing for Paris on the 6am train with Father Duffy, leaving the Parisian restaurants and the throb of life there. I also recall the beauty of the neat, peaceful countryside. The invader was very near, but we had stopped him and were already driving him back. I would be hard pushed to tell how I spent my time in the luxurious big city, in that lively, generous but decadent heart of France. On July 23rd, I had slept in my double bed in the chateau for the last time, before a great, dangerous battle – and I knew it. What delight those hours of rest were before danger! But I also had such regrets, because I had not spent that day strolling about the fields, meditating, collecting my thoughts or writing to my family.

In the room next to mine were two American officers for whom I had got a billet. I knocked at their door to say good night. I went in – what a scene! How like men from Antiquity this race of fine athletes was, at the same time primitive and civilised! These two fellows were lying completely naked, side by side, on the double bed. In the moonlight, I could see their handsome, vigorous bodies gleaming white and healthy in the pale rays of the moon. They were conversing, savouring the soft warm night air in a way Europeans could not have done because they are too 'civilised'. Not a single German or Frenchman would have dared to pose so casually in front of a witness. The Americans are not prudish. They do not try to hide their bodies; on the contrary, they are proud of them. They do not feel the often ludicrous embarrassment of present-day Europeans. In fact, they are healthier than we are because they behave more naturally. These two young athletes, so proud of their good looks, did not move or feel even slightly ill-at-ease when I went in; so, after saying good night I left them to go on talking of their fiancées, their country, their university. Would it not be highly desirable for us to learn this absence of prudishness and this pride in one's physical beauty? It is as though some of the Greek soul has been passed on to the democracy of the Americans: uncomplicated morals, love of strength and beauty, these are American characteristics. Don't let us make fun of these unsophisticated people who can sometimes be more honest than we are, and who can teach us long-forgotten ancient truths

After this lengthy digression, I must return to my subject. Before describing the battle I wanted to bring out one of these contrasts which are so frequent in a combatant's life. One evening it is happiness, life with its brilliance and passion; the next morning it might be death. At last we relieved the French on the 25th, with the usual disparity in numbers: our thousand men relieved two hundred. In fact, as I pointed out to the Colonel, we had relieved two decimated battalions of very distressed troops with our one battalion. During the morning of the 26th, the Colonel and I went to reconnoitre the sector near Beuvardes. Thus we were able to decide where to place our reserve battalions. We found the French colonel in the front line at the edge of a small wood, at the bottom of a valley one kilometre south of Beuvardes; his lines stretched along a small brook in the woods just east of the village. The Colonel was very tense, and pricked up his ears like a frightened battle horse whenever a shell hissed overhead from the north of the Forêt de Fère and crashed noisily on the village to our left. Colonel McCoy and I studied the lanes round about to make sure that the relief battalions would not be seen, in case Ridge 228, north of Beuvardes, was still occupied by the enemy – something nobody knew.

So, in broad daylight on the 26th, we relieved the French who were going to the rear and, during the night, we relieved those going to that part of the Forêt de Fère south east of Beuvardes. Anderson was in the front line due west of Courpoil as early as the 26th. On the morning of that day the Colonel and I had reconnoitered the terrain and for the whole afternoon we were at Courpoil under an artillery bombardment. Then, when we returned from the front line, we tried to find a site for our headquarters. I had used my influence to delay the movement of our headquarters for twenty-four hours. We chose the last house in Courpoil on the Beuvardes road opposite a tall avenue of poplars. We had an excellent view of the terrain occupied by the enemy, but the house also stood out conspicuously. Fortunately one could reach it, unseen, from Ridge 228. The Brigade Headquarters was also in the village, and by one of those miracles that were so frequent, shells dropped there without causing much damage. The Colonel and I went to report to the brigade in the thick of German fire, and we had to crawl, making ridiculous attempts to shelter behind mud walls. What a lot of walking we did that day, what a lot of kilometres we covered, often needlessly! Not only had we seen the French colonel in the front line at Beuvardes in the morning, but also before that, the colonel in command of the brigade, a good man who had chosen a position under a few beautiful poplars which served as roof and shelter. We had found a spot for our 3rd Battalion, which had become redundant because Donovan had enough troops to relieve two French battalions. Finally we had raced under shell fire to pay our respects to Brigadier General Lenihan

That same day I witnessed an amusing incident that could have become tragic. Our headquarters was established in Courpoil as early as midday on the 26th, before our troops came up. As I was ravenous, I pretended I needed information from the nearest French Major whom Anderson was to relieve; I set off and was lucky enough to come across a friendly major, a former cavalryman, at the battalion headquarters, where I was served the left-overs of the meal. I was completely exhausted, very much on edge because I was tired, hungry and had not had enough sleep. I bless that major for the meal that he favoured me with! I don't know how my Americans managed: I am sure the Colonel at the Brigade Headquarters only had tea and a few biscuits.

The sector was not yet in American hands, but you could see that the heroic, muddle-headed army was arriving.

Right in the middle of the afternoon, a Service Corps unit from the 117th Engineers (our divisional Engineers) came and settled under the screen of trees across from our headquarters. Half an hour later, the enemy started firing systematically, targeting their fire on the poor animals – mules and horses – tied to the trees. At first it was funny: the animals reared up, the men were frightened and fled. Then it became less funny, as the Germans poured a great number of shells on the line of trees. Fortunately this was parallel to the front so that a sweeping action was impossible, but our building was caught in the bombardment, hit squarely by 125s. It was as well that the walls were built of stone. Lieutenant Mitchell, Anderson and I and the other officers stoically awaited death in one of the ground-floor rooms. The house had a cellar which would have easily held us, but of course I could not be the one to suggest running down to the cellar. I cannot remember how it ended, but the German guns stopped. The animals were removed from their exposed position and from all the din. As it turned out, two men were slightly wounded in our headquarters; not a single animal was hit. But what a mindless waste of nervous energy!

At Courpoil more than anywhere else, I became aware of the immense chasm between the Americans and the French in military organisation. I was with a colonel who did not get fed, nor did our men who received hardly any supplies because the field kitchen arrived very late on the night of the 26th. The sector got cluttered up and the roads were congested as soon as the Americans arrived. This surprised my Colonel: 'Is this how it works in a French sector?' he exclaimed, forgetting that it was the sector of an American army corps we had just entered, and *we* were causing the mess. When I left our Courpoil headquarters in search of the French major – under some pretext, but mostly intending to get treated to lunch somewhere – I came across a platoon of *Poilus* sitting in holes in the woods, each in his own shelter, cheerful, fresh and rested, with large platefuls of delicious-looking vegetables in their tins. Their young officer wanted to be the one to take me to the major, but he lost his way. As we wandered about for over an hour I lost my temper, and to crown it all the wood was shelled. Yet how kind that young lieutenant was, and how patient! Without a word, he put up with my grumpy remarks and sarcasm about his knowledge of topography. Eventually he brought me back to his platoon, and this time a *Poilu* took me to the major without losing his

33

way. But what a spirit of quiet dedication and close cooperation I saw at all levels! As an army, my Americans amounted to nothing. They were a poor bunch compared with the harmonious discipline and heroism of the French regiment.

We spent the night at the Château d'Epieds again, planning to finish organising our headquarters in Courpoil at daybreak. Indeed there was hardly anything we could do while relief was taking place in the later part of the night of the 26th. Then followed that memorable day, the 27th. When I recall these events I feel it might all have been a dream. My 1:80,000 Ordnance Survey map is full of meaning for me: short pencil strokes represent our lines, which the French Command knew so little about; for it is a fact that in an offensive one doesn't know where the front line is, to within a kilometre. Is a village held by the French or the Germans? No one knows, even those most closely involved. In one place there is a gap in the line which whole battalions could squeeze through; in another there is a salient. Needless to say it is even more true of the Americans than of ours. In what intense moment, all geared up for action, did I draw these pencil strokes?

Briefly the events flash through my mind and I relive them. I am wearing my uniform, carrying my cumbersome equipment, field-glasses, revolver, haversack, gas mask, flask, maps. And my right arm is in a sweat, tired from the weight of my sky-blue greatcoat, which I use as a blanket at night. My helmet, which is too big, presses down uncomfortably on my head. I can see again the brilliant July sun, and I am racing, rushing feverishly across the fields where the Germans have hurriedly started and then abandoned the rye harvest. I can see myself deep in the mêlée once more. For a moment, I feel again that disagreeable sensation of ever-present danger. Sometimes walking, sometimes running, I carry out my many duties, reconnoitering the lines and liaising, through the clumps of trees and bushes and short-cut lanes, and forest glades with their dry grass. I can see the houses in Courpoil again, the orchards not too damaged by bullets, and the devastated, looted homes of the good people who fled. How far away and unreal it all seems! With its beautiful light and living rays the July sun beats down on this scene, and seems a silent reproach to man and his brutality. It is ideal weather for war, and of course nature is, as always, indifferent: never were there more beautiful or better days to live and love than in that month of July.

The French Command didn't know whether Beuvardes was still occupied by the enemy. We had been there, then we had evacuated the village amid bursts of heavy gunfire and gas shells. As early as the 26th I was certain it was no longer occupied, because when I was at the French lieutenant colonel's headquarters east of Beuvardes, I had witnessed the shelling of the village, around 1p.m. On the 27th, in our Courpoil headquarters we were without news for a long time. From the middle of the road, a bit further down, we could see the hills behind Beuvardes, but nothing was happening there; it was dead calm. Not a single shell had been fired on Courpoil since the afternoon of the 26th; the relief by our front line battalion during the night had been uneventful. As early as 6a.m. we had left our billiard room (!) and were settled in Courpoil.

We tried unsuccessfully to make contact with Major Donovan, who was nowhere to be found. For over 24 hours we had lost track of him as he strolled around the front line, accompanied by his men, with typical American courage. But with equal American *insouciance* he had failed to inform his Colonel of his whereabouts. From then on we lost the 1st Battalion. We didn't even have time to set up the phone lines, for the silence indicated that the enemy was retreating. Unknown to us our 1st Battalion, under Major Donovan, had started pursuing them. He was unaware that the latest orders given out changed the axis of his march! Thus they finally ended on the far right of the division (we were on its left wing) on the evening of the 27th, after presenting the German artillery with a fine target by their flanking movement and causing a few unnecessary casualties. As early as 9a.m., we suspected the Boche were retreating. We sent an officer in his sidecar to reconnoitre Beuvardes and the hills beyond. This was unsuccessful, for we did not see him and his sidecar again until much later. He probably did what he fancied, reconnoitering the 166th regiment which, on our left as he told us, was relieving a French division, This was precisely the one that had trained us in the Forêt de Paroy (14th *Chasseurs*, led by Colonel Dussauges).

By 10a.m., I was growing very impatient: a French cyclist, a cavalryman on a bike, came and asked for permission to go to Beuvardes to visit his parents' house. In the evening of the 26th, during the lull in the German shelling, which lasted all night and marked the prelude to the enemy's retreat, we saw, walking through Courpoil from the direction of Beuvardes, a wretched, pathetic procession of old men and women. Those poor people were overjoyed to have been liberated, and were walking cheerfully beneath the weight of their treasured possessions. But how pale and gaunt their faces were! They had lived between the two fronts for two or three days, subjected to attacks from both sides, even gas shells. They had lived in their cellars, trembling under the heavy German bombardment. That evening I noticed that bigger shells, 210s at least, had been fired, so that a number of cellars had collapsed and houses had been crushed. Those poor people had left their houses the day before they were liberated, and I think they suffered the very last shelling of Beuvardes. We allowed the cavalryman to ride to his native village.

Eventually, about noon, seeing there were no more returning from Beuvardes, we gave an order to the 3rd Battalion who were south of the Forêt de Fère, camping in a small copse and very comfortable on former German sites. As Donovan had gone at an angle, leaving our front line exposed we ordered the 3rd Battalion to follow on the heels of the Germans, along the original axis,. Anderson was to follow. As for me, I decided that before setting off I must have something to eat. I went to find an artillery headquarters very near to ours and ordered lunch for the Colonel, the chaplain, me and the others. Preston soon got back with Lieutenant Colonel Mitchell. Both were exhausted after spending many useless hours in search of Major Donovan. They informed us that his battalion had set off to the north east, a direction which would take him to the sector of Croix Rouge Farm, i.e. the sector reserved for the167th and 168th, and commanded by General MacArthur since 10 July. We ate very heartily, especially the Colonel who had not had anything for a very long time. I paid for this out of my own pocket, as indeed I should do. During the meal, Colonel McCoy had the idea of sending for his food supply company. I must admit that for once I was wrong: I opposed him, because I still didn't believe in the German retreat of which we had no certain knowledge, and I was still shaken by the shelling of the 117th Engineers the evening before. I was furious but the Colonel rightly ignored my angry protest. To my knowledge this was one of the rare circumstances when an American displayed some insight. Colonel McCoy was very quick-tempered and jealous of his authority. Opposing him publicly caused him a lot of irritation and this provoked a scathing reply from him, which I admit I deserved.

Soon after this, around 2pm, we found the 3rd Battalion, led by Major McKenna, marching in strict formation along the Beuvardes-Fère road. Not the slightest preliminary reconnaissance had been undertaken. On receiving the order to advance in pursuit of the enemy, McKenna had simply set off without making any combat preparations. I was deeply shocked, worse – terrified. It so happened that McKenna was right and the enemy had retreated, quickly falling back several kilometres, but what a terrible risk it was for a battalion of 1000 men! I must admit I was somewhat overcautious on the 27th. But looking back on the events of the 26th, how justified my fears were!

On our left the French were relieved by Colonel Hough's people. This left a hopeless mix-up. I don't know if the American and French staff headquarters had agreed this beforehand, or who was responsible. Be that as it may, the battalions of the 166th Regiment soon became entangled with ours. Colonel McCoy intervened and stopped them, which caused an argument with Captain Lawrence, the French liaison officer at the 166th. Furthermore we found, about level with Préaux Farm, that the axis of the 10th Colonial Regiment was also crossing ours. All these movements converged on Fère-en-Tardenois with remarkable inaccuracy and regrettable overlapping. As a result, we later found at Villers-sur-Fère, in our sector, a line of French troops who had set up camp after us during the night of the 27th. But at least we managed to ensure that the 166th were kept in reserve. They intervened only in the afternoon of the 28th, at Colonel McCoy's request.

It may be difficult for an army corps headquarters to coordinate effectively the movements of a number of divisions on irregular terrain along a shrinking front. Some of these divisions are stationary, simply waiting, whilst others are advancing smoothly. All the same I have no doubt that avoiding errors in moving troops must be possible. This is one of the reasons why senior officers in infantry regiments have to be intelligent as well as brave. If you work in harmony with fellow officers, you get men to spread out rather than packing them together. The front is reinforced without exposing vulnerable masses or clusters. It is ready to function like a spring, not a heavy, massive obstacle, which would be easily broken if attacked. Just try and break the front of a division that is reinforced by a carefully spaced rear section: after the advanced posts, you will be caught in the crossfire from reserve positions. Colonel McCoy realised this, and on that day he acted like a real soldier – not only did he get the 166th removed from our path, but he went to Préaux Farm to discuss things with the battalion leader and the colonial troops, and we agreed on everybody's role.

Never as much as in those days at Château Thierry did I realise how exciting war is: men like danger and the deadly game of war. It is true that there are too many dangers in the infantry, and for a *Poilu* common sense eventually prevails over the mindless excitement of the beginning. But this war of movement was going to bring out my spirit of adventure again. After four years of a static, cautious war, I felt pleasure – not unadulterated, it is true, because danger always is an unpleasant experience – but pleasure undeniably, as when entering enemy ground and finding the traces of a hasty retreat at every step. At Beuvardes we waited for a few hours before informing the brigade of our advance, and the colonel was able to send for his car. About 5p.m., we set off in the valiant little Ford. Everything went well until we reached Préaux Farm, but from then on, we had to use dirt tracks which the 1:80,000 map showed only imperfectly after a few months of German occupation. It is extraordinary how quickly changes occur on a terrain where all sorts of convoys circulate. I was soon to find out that the Forêt de Fère had been made into a gigantic arsenal: enormous stocks of ammunition of all calibres, gas shells, long 150s, 210s, even larger calibres, huge Navy brass cases, were piled everywhere under the trees. I only realised on my return, a few days later, that the Château Thierry salient was an immense triangle crammed with men and ammunition. Had the third German attack on Epernay-Rheims-Châlons succeeded, it would have become immediately a starting base towards Paris – what else were these enormous supplies for? I had never seen the like of this, even when we launched an offensive.

We found our 2nd Battalion level with Préaux Farm. Later, towards the close of the day, we hurried a bit more. We nearly got stuck and lost our way in mud tracks some 100 metres from Préaux Farm. We had to get out, push the car, fill a rut with branches, corrugated iron and other such material, and only managed to get through with great difficulty. The maze of mud roads, intersected by tracks going to the Ferme de l'Espérance, became more manageable as soon as we got out of the marshy area north-west of the Forêt de Fère. We stopped for a moment at the farm, which was concealed from enemy view in a slight fold. I still have the picture of the whole area present in my memory: our front battalion was barely coming abreast of us. I recall the orchard around the farm and the silence hovering over the scene. Nearby was a small pond surrounded by willows with their cool shade. On the hilltops over the Ourcq, north of the farm, a forest screened us from the enemy. They must have stopped north of the small stream. We could hear a few of their shells dropping in the valley, probably on the village of Villers-sur-Fère.

One of the most amusing encounters I had in the war took place at the Ferme de l'Espérance. Colonel McCoy saw a group of French cavalrymen, and we stopped them for news. To my surprise I recognised the sergeant patrol leader, *'Hello, Caburet, how are you? Don't you recognise an old school-friend?'* He was even more surprised than I was to meet an old childhood friend in an

American sector. He had come to liaise with Major McKenna, whom I pointed out to him. I arranged to meet him the next day at the Ferme de l'Espérance, but I was not able to go to the farm again and I don't think he did either. We had thought of making it our headquarters, but McCoy had bolder ideas: it was too far from the Ourcq, and we didn't know where the Germans would stop. We therefore pressed on a bit further, along roads that had been cleared of all human traces since the Germans had been through, and we came upon the Château de la Forêt only a moment later. It was getting darker, but July evenings are long, and it is still light more than an hour after the sun has gone down. The château provided a magnificent shelter, just right for a command post. Upstairs was peaceful and luxurious, and the cellars had been well fitted out by the enemy, with divan-bases and all the comfort required. The only drawback was that the entrance to the château, on the main road to Fère, was in full sight of the heights north of the Ourcq, and therefore could not be approached from the front. We visited the first houses at Villers-sur-Fère, a village over one kilometre long and taking up the whole southern slope of the valley. We could see that it was empty, but we gave ourselves the little thrill of patrolling the deserted streets in our car. We decided to set up our command post at the Château de la Forêt.

Naturally, as we had the use of a car we had to go and report to General Lenihan at Beuvardes. That was our undoing. Had Colonel McCoy simply been content to stay with his troops, had he not been ambitious, seeking the esteem and notice of his superiors, we could have set ourselves up peacefully in the château. General Lenihan would not then have had the absurd idea of installing himself in this wasps' nest. The general was so enthusiastic when he heard of the château that he immediately decided to move his headquarters there. I couldn't say anything. My idea had been to set up the regimental position there because, deep down, I was firmly determined to keep a close watch, and place sentries preventing activity on the road and in front of the château. But Lenihan arrived, and the place was soon packed with hundreds of liaison men, divisional first aid posts, etc. Men from the brigade were stationed by candlelight in the rooms facing the enemy. A few shells dropped and frightened them: this soon got them to take measures showing a prudence that was even more ridiculous than their stupid lack of foresight. Even in the cellars no one dared so much as to light a cigarette or to turn lights on in the rooms looking out to the forest. This unfortunate whim of a childish, thought-less general, trying to make a noble gesture by being stationed among his troops *and* in a château, was to cost the lives of scores of men killed by shells around the château, and most of all massacred by air raids. Worse still, the general would be forced to flee in a panic, as indeed we were, on the Ourcq, the next day, the 28th of July.

During the evening of the 27th nobody had any food. Instead of taking a rest, we spent the night in our car between Beuvardes and Villers-sur-Fère, on roads that were cluttered up and blocked by the artillery. At the château, no sooner had the general arrived than orders came to attack the northern banks of the Ourcq, *'Without artillery preparation, at daybreak'*; orders that went against one of the main teachings we had tried to instill into the Americans. In this, their first battle, the headquarters of the first American army corps that ever existed ignored our experience, which we had paid for so dearly. The American army just had to show guts, to outstrip the French and, if at all possible, leave them far behind. It is unthinkable now that the pride of ambitious men who ran no risks whatsoever could have caused the deaths of thousands, and the headquarters officers who had written the criminally callous orders never felt the slightest remorse. After a sleepless night, we had to attack, and without artillery! Our troops were exhausted. Like us, our men had had neither food nor sleep. I could understand how they felt because of how I felt, even though I had not spent the day and the night with a knapsack on my back, on a march that was all the more painful as it was slow.

I went pale on hearing this order, but I still hoped there would be some reprieve. Lieutenant Colonel Mitchell rode off into the night to inform Anderson – another American idea! There was still no news of Donovan, who had wandered off several kilometres to our right and had not tried to liaise with us. I learned later that the barrage of 77s we heard around 7pm on the Ourcq valley, to the right of Villers-sur-Fère, had been dropped on him and his men. The Colonel and I went to the 3rd Battalion which was in the front line and would have the *honou*r of carrying out the unthinking order of the Allied Command Headquarters. We drove down the long main street of the village, but soon were stopped by a fallen tree. However, we eventually found the McKenna position in a small house near the school, in the centre of the village.

The memory of the hours that followed is one of the most painful of those I have of the war. We were seven or eight officers in that room and we dared not have the light on. There was only one window, but the Americans had not thought of covering it. Shells would drop on the village, very close by, every ten minutes, with a crash which the thin brick walls could not muffle. We were obliged to read our maps by torchlight behind a cupboard door. McKenna was very cheerful, although his officers were not: they were the ones who would have to cross the Ourcq river, about which we knew nothing, whether it was wide or if there were any footbridges etc. As I did not know whether the enemy was in strength on its north side, I could not say if this attack was impossible, though my attitude spoke for itself. Eventually the Colonel called back his captains at the last moment and announced that he was taking it on himself not to execute the order. I, on the other hand, had suggested that we risk just one company, and only if it got across the Ourcq should we move the rest of the battalion forward. But our Colonel's courage took a big weight off my conscience. If nobody had intervened after this, over 700 men would have been spared.

Unfortunately however, a colonel from the Corps Headquarters was with us. He was a gift from the brigade, of course. He called McCoy, took him aside and ordered him to execute the order from the Corps Headquarters. McCoy called back the captains yet again. Such is discipline: we had to obey, no matter what the cost. A moment later, at day break, Hurley Company (K Company) crossed the Ourcq at Moulin Vert under a few isolated shots. Two other companies followed, while M Company was kept in reserve. My memory of the hours that followed is unbearable. I feel as if I have dipped my hands in blood, taken part in a murder. A powerless onlooker, I saw, some 800 meters away, on the hills north of the Ourcq, among the wheat and lucerne fields, the massacre of an American battalion, my own, the one I knew and had trained behind the lines. As for our Colonel, totally improvident and thoughtless, he had placed his headquarters heedlessly on the road that ran parallel to the Ourcq south of the village, in full view of the enemy posted at Seringes and at the edge of the Forêt de Nesles. There, in the ditch, we sat piled together, officers and liaison men, Brigade Headquarters and Regiment Headquarters. A few prisoners arrived. The men from the company were crammed together under the nearby trees, with no shelter or thought of digging one. I had to make a tremendous fuss to get a small trench dug for the Colonel.

At first, the Boche did not know what had come upon them. The small posts on the Ourcq surrendered, astonished by the courage of an opponent crossing a river where water came up to the armpits. The Ourcq was neither very deep nor wide, but you had to get wet. Not a single American complained of the obstacle: they saw it as just a trickle of water, and I do not think they even tried to use the many footbridges they could still find at Moulin Vert. Half an hour later, a few shells started dropping in the area, but they were on the far right, on Sergy and the Ourcq and the valley near Sergy. Evidently the German army was not well informed about where that isolated attack came from, and indeed it became obvious that we, the165th, were the only ones attempting to cross the Ourcq. The Colonel informed the brigade, who ordered the 166th, on our left, to advance; but it was only the next day that they finally did so, towards Seringe et Nesles, thus showing much more prudence and common sense than my daring Irishmen.

About 7a.m., it became obvious that our troops were unable to advance. We could see the companies, in thin lines of skirmishers, lying in the wheat. Every time they stood up they were caught sideways by machine-gun fire from the left, where none of our troops was covering them. Colonel McCoy ordered Anderson and a machine-gun company to advance down the valley of the Rut du Pont Brûlé, but being down below and wrongly positioned, the machine-gunners and Anderson were useless. Yet the battalion that had been given the order to advance to its objective, the village of Nesles, persisted heroically. Soon, around 8a.m., the rattling of the machine-guns became fearsome. The plateau was swept incessantly; the German barrage became more accurate and started dropping just a few shells, to start with, in the wheat and the lucerne where our men were. The endless procession of the wounded came past, accompanied by fugitives, since each wounded man was a lucky opportunity for two Americans to take their comrade to the rear. Seething with rage, I watched this bloody procession, among which I recognised a few faces. McKenna moved to the Moulin Vert wood by the river. Nothing was being resolved. The Colonel got over the excitement of the first advance. I advised falling back on the Ourcq, and at about 10am the Colonel gave the order.

The enemy artillery became very active. I went and lay down in a house in the village but was soon driven out by hails of shells. I have never been able to stay awake for two days, even in a war. I was tired out and could not keep my eyes open. I took shelter in a cellar but could not sleep, as an infernal bombardment started on the village, and the area round the church was completely destroyed after a few hours. Heavy shells threatened to bury me alive in the cellar. Indeed, there was no way I could get rest. I went out between two bursts of 130s and found the walls had crashed down round my temporary shelter. As I was coming out a burst of shells dropped and flattened a garden wall twenty metres away.

I found the McCoy headquarters in turmoil; the Colonel had taken refuge among tall poplars to the right of the village – facing the enemy. Like a thunderbolt, a shell would strike a tree now and again. Planes would fly overhead, chase and pelt us with small hand bombs. A moment later, we went back to our headquarters on the road. Major McKenna had been killed on the Ourcq during my brief, one-hour rest. News had come of the front line battalion, who had carried out the order to fall back only too well. They completely abandoned the battlefield, in disarray and *hors de combat*. Anderson and his troops however, were stretched out to the right along the sunken lane a hundred metres north of the river, which provided an excellent shelter at the front of the slope. All four captains in the McKenna battalion had been wounded, several other officers were killed; one of them was Watson, a charming, courageous young man from L Company, very unassuming and eager to learn; and Smith, a very brave man from I Company, was killed along with two others from K Company. I estimated that over 500 dead lay there on the hillside, some of them like khaki-coloured spots. In the village itself, the losses were very heavy, especially at the first aid post where shells finished off many of the wounded. No sooner were we back in our small trench by the road than a shell dropped five metres away and I was wounded in the shoulder and face. At first I thought the wound was severe, but it was only shrapnel. I persuaded the Colonel to leave this spot for another one, a sunken road I had noticed outside the village a small distance from the houses.

My wound put me in a good mood again, and gave me renewed drive and energy. I was very proud to be able to stay at my post, though wounded. My face was covered with blood but this soon dried up. We walked up the road during a lull, for hell cannot go on forever: it takes too much ammunition. On our way we met my friend Captain Jacobson the artilleryman, who mocked me gently about my wounds. 'This will earn you a nice mention in dispatches', he said, '*Stayed at his post though wounded, etc.*' He was coming to offer us the artillery's belated services – but after all, we had been ordered to attack without artillery. And although Jacobson, this young, brave Frenchman, was there, we certainly would not have seen any American artilleryman, for liaising was not a normal duty for them. It existed in theory, but hardly otherwise. I have never seen an artilleryman with a rank higher than lieutenant or captain in an American infantry headquarters unless he was a liaison officer. Artillery majors or colonels never took the trouble to come and find out if we were satisfied or what we needed, and see for themselves the terrain that had to be covered. A map was all those skilled topographers needed!

My new choice of an headquarters had not been very good at all. Arriving in the sunken lane, I saw open dressing kits and equipment, and realised the Germans had just shelled it and knocked down the trees over the road. Then I became doubtful about how efficient the protection offered by the three metre high embankment would be. However, I installed the Colonel here. The day was drawing to an end. I waited for Jacobson to finish his observation of the terrain. The road was very well situated: from there we could see the bare slopes of the Ourcq, where we had been stopped east of the Rut du Pont Brûlé. After warning the Colonel to dig in at the foot of the bank, and particularly to hide from the planes, I went up to the brigade first aid post for my wounds to be seen to. The Château de la Forêt was in turmoil, under the harassing fire of 150s. Fortunately, only a small area was affected. Because the *château* was merely a large house, the shells would pass over it and vanish into the forest, although on their way they chipped walls and blasted window panes.

The general had just fled, or rather was in the midst of doing so, and in such a hurry to move out that he did not even speak to me. He wanted everyone to go, but in the end he left a very unhappy major with a telephone. The 165th first aid post was still in the cellar, but I was attended to in one of the ground floor rooms just after a lull: they had not managed to find a safe place for the treatment room. I was given a tetanus jab and a small antiseptic dressing, which cannot have been antiseptic, as my shoulder wound soon became infected. However, I fell into a blissful sleep on one of the divan-bases in the cellar. Preston was there and had been there all day, poor fellow! He was completely exhausted after the various missions he had been entrusted with. I told him where the Colonel was, but advised him to have a rest, for there was nothing left to be done in the village for the moment.

That night I had an excellent sleep. Having begged for a bit of food from the brigade field kitchen, who at first turned me down (*'You are from the 165th, go get yourself fed there'*), I went back down to Villers-sur-Fère and found the Colonel in the cellar. It appeared that a lot had happened at the Sunken Lane Headquarters: a shell had hit two officers, one of whom (Cane) had died. From then on, the war became an ordinary static war again. The protection provided in our headquarters was only an illusion; it was a washroom on the ground-floor of a house with a concrete ceiling: a 77 would have gone through it! But I had to admire the cleverness of the officer who had lodged the colonel there,

44

when I found out that this same captain, a good man, but canny and very American, had been occupying with his men a very solid, well-fitted-out headquarters close by. However, as a few shells dropped near us the next day and a few men were wounded, we had to move and find another cellar.

What a life in that headquarters! The house, crammed with people, was a little shack which a 150mm shell would have crushed to the ground. Its only advantage was that it stood slightly away from the village and near a large drinking trough in which cool, clear water was flowing. I remember that I quenched my thirst there many times, and even once had a full bath – not a very pleasant experience, for when I least expected them a few shells forced me to hasten my ablutions. We were in a kind of hollow shaded with poplars, on the right of the village as you went down to the Ourcq. The hollow was of no advantage to us, because it was soon hit by several mustard gas shells which affected us more in this new lower position.

It was on the 29th when I found the Colonel so sumptuously installed; the telephone was working. Donovan had arrived, and with his usual drive had retaken the terrain abandoned the day before, using the excellent cover provided by the little valley of the Rut de la Ferme Meurcy. He and his men were occupying the Cola wood, left of the brook, and the slopes were filled with our two battalions, the 1st and 2nd. There was no reserve except the remainder of the 3rd, which had re-formed in the village and lodged in cellars with the *Hors Rang* company. Furthermore, Meaney, the one captain who had escaped the massacre, had only two hundred and fifty men with him. A number of fugitives had slipped away under the pretext of wounds or shell concussion, but most of all because they had no officers left, no one to command them. The Machine-gun Company had completely disappeared, for at the moment when it was gathering by the Château de la Forêt on the evening of the 28th, a German plane dropped a bomb right in the middle of them, killing and wounding about twenty men. Terror-stricken, the others had fled.

Although army police blocks are indispensable at the rear of any fighting unit, none had been set up in our sector. Colonel McCoy was indignant about this and informed the Division Headquarters with commendable honesty. Only a handful of men from the 3rd Battalion were left, and instead of being used wisely, this small number of survivors was horribly misused and sacrificed by the Colonel. Here I no longer had the power I previously exercised in the Champagne defensive campaign. The Colonel had put me in my place several times, and I was obliged to be persuasive and to ask for things in roundabout ways. McCoy was impulsive and gave his orders on the spur of the moment. Should a request for ammunition come from Anderson or Donovan, he would immediately send thirty of Meaney's men to resupply the line in broad daylight, not thinking that the ammunition would never get there, as it was under enemy fire in full sight of its artillery. Meaney told me that one of these groups was completely wiped out. The Americans did not know how to move under fire. During a bombardment they would wait with a casual attitude that was senseless rather than brave, instead of using cover. They would stay in the dangerous area, hiding as an ostrich does with its head in the sand, some behind trees, others behind bushes. In those days at the Ourcq, I saw resupplying parties remaining passive, like brainless sheep, behind a line of poplars, waiting for an order from their leader.

Beneath the veneer of apparent order the headquarters was in complete disorder. Having a rest or lying down was impossible. We had visitors from behind the lines. People would come to show that they had been there – after the battle, mark you, when the danger was over. We received ceaseless calls from the front line, or we called Donovan or Anderson, mostly Donovan. We stayed in this washroom on the 29th, 30th and 31st, and I had nothing else to do but to observe the muddle-headedness of the Americans, their spirited, but hasty impetuosity in action. They never reflected or planned. Instead of asking the front line to wait patiently for the supplies, they would straightaway carry out Donovan's eccentric orders for reinforcements or fatigue parties – all this in broad daylight. Waiting till evening to place the 37s, reinforce the machine-guns and so on, had occurred to no-one. It was no use telling them: everyone was over-agitated, Merle-Smith especially.

I have mentioned Merle-Smith before. He was the tall captain from I Company, ex-cavalryman, intelligent and cultured, whom I had admired in the training period at Baissey. I had always been on his side, particularly when the Colonel supported McKenna to replace Monoyan when the latter was dismissed. But this was in vain, for McKenna was Irish-American and his brother was the Colonel's right-hand man, who held the threads of a thousand little intrigues that spread out beyond the headquarters into the companies and battalions. Yes, the Irish did make a close group. Captain McKenna became the major of the 3rd Battalion. Poor man! This was tragically unlucky for him, as he was killed on the 28th. What skillful schemers those McKennas were, what braggarts! It was McKenna who would write boastful letters, blazing with patriotism, to American newspapers after the first days in the Lorraine sector, when the 1st Battalion had been hit by two shells! The McKenna-Donovan party, or clique, prevailed over Merle-Smith who was affiliated to nobody. In the end, Merle-Smith, who had been wounded on the 28th by a bullet in his elbow, remained at his station with dignity and courage. I still remember that he came to the Colonel in the middle of the day on the 28th, with no company left, to get orders for the 3rd Battalion. This tall fellow never turned a hair when 150s smashed trees not far from him; he looked a fine figure and, with a smile on his face, would describe to me his crossing of the Ourcq, when he had water up to his armpits – and he was at least 6ft 3in tall. His lighter was wet; he could not light it because the tinder was damp and his left elbow was racked with pain. With a comical look he asked me to light his cigarette as a friendly favour. That was real sangfroid under fire. I must admit lighting a cigarette was the least of my worries at that moment.

Finally Merle-Smith got his reward. The Colonel took him in his headquarters as officer in charge of operations. However, it was very disappointing for me to see him at work. He became unbearable, stopped having any food or rest; day and night he would stay on the phone over trivialities, communicating useless orders, forever asking for information of which we had no need. We liaised with the artillery, however, and we even had a visit from a liaison officer, which was very useful. Merle-Smith also looked after the infantrymen, and he pestered the artillery so that we got them to bombard the enemy frequently, mostly thanks to his and the Colonel's insistence. But what a useless waste of ammunition it sometimes was! The Colonel and Merle-Smith had pictured the German line without knowing anything about it, except through vague information from Major Donovan, who was at the bottom of the slope and not thinking much about observing the enemy. At night we would imagine machine-gun positions whenever Donovan's men heard the slightest rattling. Once we even went so far as to ask for counter-battery fire on imaginary guns behind the German lines. The naiveté in those people's minds, intoxicated by their role, the wonderful tactical stories they elaborated – it was quite a spectacle. Nobody thought of living a normal life, of resting, eating and drinking. They were busy, that was all that mattered. As for resupplying the front line, I think I was the only one who thought of it. A meal was cooked for them by the Meaney Battalion and the Support Company. But we heard later that no food had reached the companies in the front line. Only the 2nd Battalion and the second line got the meal.

On the 29th in the afternoon, Colonel McCoy wanted to go to the front line to see how his people were getting on. His aide, McA (I forget his name), did not even offer to accompany him. I had to stand up, of course. Everybody fell silent. Nobody offered to go up with the Colonel except me. McA tried to find a good guide for the Colonel. What a noble effort! This self-interest prevailed in the thick of war. Nobody would put themselves out for the Colonel: everyone to his own job. No one at the headquarters was interested in what was happening in the front line. I felt very indignant. Later, when passing by the church I was pleased to notice the fine, tall stature and calm face of Duffy, our chaplain. I shook hands with him affectionately, but the Colonel didn't stop. We found that things had got hot for those of our men who advanced along the Rut du Pont Brûlé. A bullet had hit Donovan's hand and his aide Ames was killed by his side. Donovan stayed at his command post with his bandaged hand. Although a mediocre leader, he was brave and had powerful influence. That day his achievement was to infiltrate the enemy positions using the cover of the valley; and at the same time he was obeying the Colonel's orders.

After crossing the stream at the Pont-Moulin, after a fairly violent barrage which dropped on the battalions of the 166th on our left, we found clusters of men from the 2nd Battalion along the river. I have never seen such a mass of people crammed together. Fortunately the slope gave good protection and hid them from sight, but not a single officer had the wit to make space between his men and get them to dig individual foxholes. These men were clustered together, needlessly waiting for death. I reprimanded the officers of the 1st Battalion, and made the same comments to them twenty-four hours later, when I visited the sector with Jacobson. It was during the visit with McCoy that I met on these slopes my friend Lawrence Irving whom I advised to space out his men and get them to dig trenches. The Colonel behaved very well that day. We spent the whole evening visiting our men and talking with Major Donovan and other officers.

American courage has not the same quality as French courage. It is more theatrical, less deep. It is physical endurance rather than courage: really the Yank's attitude in war is a bit like that of a good sportsman, a boxer who endures all the permitted blows without a word. I shall come back to this when I try to gather together all the scattered reflections I have written on the American character. In fact, one found none of the noble moral conscience of the French officer or Poilu behind the sacrifice accepted by the American soldier. American courage has been much admired but it has not always been remarkable. It was spontaneous and personal, to be sure, but sometimes a group behaved well only when the leaders were present. On the 28th for example, the 3rd Battalion remained under fire until the moment they collapsed. Standing up, the men would advance as the whistle blew, as in manoeuvres, and lie flat when they heard the fast rattle of the Maxims. They were disciplined and obeyed orders automatically. Yet an hour later the battalion had fled in disarray. Such extremes did not exist with the French. Behind the lines, American artillerymen were not ashamed to run away in large numbers, abandoning their position as soon as a shell fell too near – the French would never have done this. The Americans were not moved by a sense of duty. They were brave, but I wonder how long they would have resisted in defence.

My battalion in Champagne was an exception: we were assimilated by the French, trained and flanked by them. However, one lesson had been taught too well: you had to hold out and sacrifice yourself. But in normal circumstances, on an offensive front for example, the idea that retreating is a betrayal was not commonly held; it was completely unknown. On the 30th, Jacobson and I witnessed real panic in the 1st Battalion because someone had seen a few Germans stirring: straight away a whole army was thought to be attacking us. I was with Jacobson at Donovan's command post when the latter rushed to the phone to summon artillery fire, unaware that it was only a few men panicking. Fortunately the line was cut off and the artillery did not see us signalling for a barrage. On the 31st there was yet another panic: Donovan was clamouring for reinforcements, but I advised the Colonel to turn him down. We had 250 men left in the village and I got him to send only half of them. Then that same order was countermanded, and I hinted to the Colonel that Donovan was tense and exhausted. We therefore decided to relieve him instead of helping him! The Boche had no thoughts of attacking.

Admittedly I have met some gallant American officers. Merle-Smith was brave: on two occasions he was wounded at the front but refused to leave. The first time, in a quiet sector, was when his eardrum was perforated by shrapnel from a mine. The other time, on the Ourcq, he persisted in staying near the Colonel, in spite of his swollen, paralysed arm. Colonel McCoy was brave too, in his own way. Donovan was rash and foolhardy. To my knowledge he was wounded three times, twice lightly when on the Ourcq, and once more severely, on the Argonne, on 12 October. But their bravery did not spring from any noble sentiments for the cause of their country, or their unit. It was theatrical and sportsmanlike. I admit Donovan's great calm made him a remarkable leader of his unit, but how did he ever become a colonel? His recklessness had disastrous consequences, bringing about the massacre of men.

On the 28th, I went to the front with Jacobson, the French artillery captain, to reconnoitre the German line, as it had been decided that this time we would attack with artillery support. In two or three hours we gathered more information than had been sent by the Americans in three days. From the northern edge of the Colas wood I located the first and second German lines behind their thin barbed-wire screen. I noted the positions of machine-guns by using the observations of the men and officers in the line – nobody had done this work before us. It could have been the basis of good artillery preparation if we had been able to attack and if the Germans had not pre-empted us with their sudden retreat.

At this point I should mention that among the prisoners taken by Donovan on the 29th was a man from the Metz region of Lorraine who spoke excellent French. This was astonishing[9].

Soon the relief of the 1st Battalion was to take place at midnight on the 31st. The previous night had been troubled: resupplying was very difficult as an unremitting barrage dropped on the Ourcq. The relief night was quieter. Worn out by several sleepless nights we all had a good rest in our new headquarters, a fine cellar with divan-bases, and enough room for everybody. It was delightful. In the previous headquarters there had not been enough space on the concrete floor of the cellar; everyone lay side by side, jumbled up together. Once I even took refuge in a neighbouring house. Captain Morgan, from the Ravit Company, had favoured us with a visit and simply took my place on the floor. I was so honoured!

In war the crucial moment comes when you most relax your attention, and this is why organising life on the front is one of the most important aspects. The morning of August 1st found us fast asleep in our cellar. No artillery fire. A strange silence all night, apart from a few sniper shots. Donovan had been replaced by Meaney with his exhausted battalion, reduced by 700 dead, wounded and missing. Although the Colonel had sent the order to patrol energetically and not to lose contact with the enemy, the patrols probably did not get far, and by morning the Germans had all gone. Eventually we realised this, and by 9a.m. we already knew, or at least had a hunch, when MacArthur, Commander of the 84th Brigade since July 4th, came into our cellar and to our embarrassment announced that the Boche had departed!

I shall now give an account of the pursuit of the enemy. That day, August 1st, was our last day on the front. After the tough times at Villers-sur-Fère it was a great relief and a great joy to start our forward march again. War favours the spirit of adventure; it gives free expression to this innate boldness which even the most timorous of men do not lack. Climbing back into the little Ford was a delight: it had spent the whole time of the battle near the tree that had stopped us the first night and blocked the road. Several bits of shrapnel had broken the windows and damaged the bodywork; but on the whole, it was not too bad. We had to go and find the bridge at Fère-en-Tardenois to cross the Ourcq. The Germans were firing at the station, probably using large-calibre shells. We could hear the swishing from a great distance.

How strange it felt to drive over the terrain which the enemy had been clinging to so desperately a few hours before! The rear of the lines has always had a kind of fascination for me, since the far-off days in Lorraine, when I tried to imagine our opponents' lines through the letters I found in the knapsacks of the wounded and dead Germans. I do not think there was any hatred between the soldiers in the two camps, yet in officers' circles it was the done thing to curse the Germans and to claim you were full of hate for them; and you almost succeeded in cultivating those feelings artificially. But the suffering was the same on both sides, totally and inevitably taking over the minds of the combatants, so that the adversity and miseries we had in common created a sort of kinship between the two sides. No, we did not hate the Germans; it was impossible to spend weeks facing men who were as unhappy as we were, sacrificing themselves for the same futile reasons, without a feeling of compassion coming over you, the same compassion for them as for yourself. Mankind was overwhelmed by the horrible fate which it had imposed on itself.

I can remember driving again up the road which climbed the slopes of the Ourcq between Fère and Seringes et Nesles. In my mind I can see the corn fields, lanes, copses, the beautiful little valley with its Rut du Pont Brûlé, the ruined village of Seringes et Nesles and the medieval Nesles tower in the distance, to the right of the Forêt de Nesles. All this had been firmly held a few hours before by the enemy clinging to the terrain. Each fold had a hidden danger for us, such as that watering-place in a dip, masked from our sight by a hedge, from where a German machine-gun had caused us so much harm.

The Germans were clever at hiding and taking advantage of the smallest bushes and undulations. Their line did not go through the village, but immediately behind it on the hill, and was hidden by the houses. In front of the forest, it went down towards Meurcy Farm, concealed in slight hollows which screened it from us; a broken, zig-zagging line, a succession of deep holes camouflaged with high corn in the fields, grass elsewhere. The holes themselves were carefully covered with grass and concealed everything but the heads and shoulders of their occupants. This lethal spot was ravaged by our shells, but earlier the deadly hail from the German machine-guns had killed so many. In the Forêt de Nesles, as in that of Fère, stacked-up ammunition, traces of the German offensive, feverishly prepared but so fortunately turned into hasty retreat, could be seen everywhere.

The Colonel set up his headquarters in the hamlet of Nesles, in the last farm, where a German platoon post had been. It could not have been comfortable occupying that farm which was devastated by shells. A whole platoon had taken precarious shelter in the cellars; the German dead had been thinly buried under a few shovelfuls of earth, a rare occurrence for our enemy. There had been a fine rain, and we had difficulty driving back to our headquarters on the slippery soil which shells had thrown up on the road. The 3rd Battalion was progressing through the wood, mostly along the edges of the forest, as we had recommended. The 2nd Battalion followed. Finally Donovan appeared around 4pm, and his theatrical entry did not fail to be a success: instead of using the cover from the forest like everybody else, he emerged on the exposed plateau with all his crowd. The artillery was advancing too, and for a moment a plane caused a nasty fright among these massed troops moving across the fields. About 4p.m. the front battalion had pushed on, level with the Château de Fère, but keeping in the woods. On our left, the 166th was advancing on the open slopes.

When we got to the ridge overlooking Mareuil to the south, we were stopped for an hour or two by a barrage of 150s which made a screen of black explosions some 200 or 300 metres away, and once again I witnessed one of those foolish, criminal mistakes that are so commonplace in war. We had stopped in the cover of the woods, but the 166th had advanced, in spite of the barrage. They advanced then drew back, and instead of quickly crossing the dangerous area, they just stopped there. The shells caused around fifty casualties. It was the most absurd thing to do: about twelve men were left dead, and in the end the artillery barrage was not broken through. Attempting to break through was heading for disaster, and there was no rush; indeed the German artillery stopped firing about 6pm, and we could then advance safely.

But our men were worn out. We were among them at about 6pm and found Meaney and his battalion, perhaps 150 to 200 men, having settled for the night in a former German camp made up of comfortable foxholes covered with sheet metal, tarred paper, and full of straw and blankets taken from the villages. I soon realised there was no way we could get those men to come out of their shelters, and the battalion would not move that night. Evidently Meaney had also decided this. The Colonel gathered the other officers of the battalion, who claimed to have been stopped by machine-guns firing from Mareuil-sur-Dôle. There were certainly no machine-guns now – assuming there ever had been any. McCoy asked for a volunteer officer to lead a reconnaissance, but not a single one came forward. I knew each of these officers and how energetic they were, but they were all tired beyond their limits, with little or no food, sleep or rest since the 27th or 28th: fighting spirit is rarely found in such conditions. I was surprised the Colonel did not accept this.

At that moment the second-in-command of the headquarters arrived and, to my indignation, also urged an immediate offensive. These men refused to see how exhausted the troops were, whereas a few words I exchanged with some officers made it obvious. On our right, the 167th had also come to a standstill. As a result of having been overtaxed and its troops squandered needlessly, the whole Division was out of action. Since as early as the morning of the 28th, the 27,000 men that composed the Rainbow Division had been engaged in the battle – an unbelievable thing to do. Even the Engineers Regiment, thrown into the mêlée on the very first day of the battle, had reinforced the Infantry. All had exhausted themselves in vain, without artillery support in the ordeal of crossing the Ourcq. The four Infantry regiments and the Engineers certainly were not spaced out to a depth of one kilometre or even 500 metres! It was a terrible mistake. In four days the Division had suffered considerable losses, reaching 50 per cent for my regiment and those of the other brigade. Only the 166th had kept up its numbers because, thanks to us, it had been held in reserve through the four hardest hours. I pleaded the cause of the 3rd Battalion to the Colonel and it was decided that the 2nd Battalion, less tired perhaps, would start the forward march again and cut through the 3rd Battalion. Our liaison messengers were starting to look for Anderson when the chief of the Brigade headquarters arrived on his horse, sweating blood and croaking with fear, to announce we would be relieved that same evening. Thus ended this battle.

Finally, I would like to describe the unforgettable scene stretching before us, as we stood near the forest, in front of our communications post on the evening of August 1st. Jacobson was looking for an artillery observation position. I walked up with him and called the Colonel so he could survey the scene of devastation presenting itself to us. At my feet, the charming village of Mareuil, falling peacefully asleep in the evening mist, stretched out almost intact. Then the Germans started firing 77s: now and again, the shells would leave a light streak of blue smoke over the peaceful red roofs as the evening silence was torn by the flash of the angry explosions, before a lull settled in for a few minutes. But most of all the sky, and the whole plain extending to the west as far as the eye could see, presented a spectacle of epic grandeur. Above us, streaked by the crimson light of the sunset, the serene, consoling dome of the northern sky spread over that immense theatre of war. A long way away, the battle still continued silently. One could not hear the slightest rumble, yet in the distance the progress of the French army was marked out by a blueish trail hanging over the ground, showing the line of the German barrage. The magic of the colours was unforgettable in this landscape ravaged by war; the beauty of nature seemed desecrated by the criminal brutality of man. Nature was protesting strongly, asserting itself in the magnificent sunset, the soft colours of the vegetation, the lush and fertile soil.

The German retreat was evident at last. On the northern horizon, which was now taking on rich, dark crimson shades, it was announced by the ammunition depots blowing up, the huge columns of smoke rising to the sky, ever renewed, billowing up and shot through by the gleam of explosions and flashes from the fires. Six or seven of these columns showed the positions of the ammunition depots. Jacobson took it as a matter of interest to locate these on the map. It *was* indeed the German retreat, and however orderly, methodical, protected by its artillery, it nonetheless involved considerable losses of ammunition and material. And what had become of their prestige and attacking spirit? Yes, it was victory indeed, and while all the shades of the evening grew deeper and darker, and a few projectiles burst very close by, I admired the enemy and his skillful retreat but I was overjoyed by his defeat, thus proclaimed to the face of the sky and the earth.

And the exhausted troops, unaware of this glory, were peacefully asleep.

Chapter 3

St. Mihiel, 12th September 1918

O<small>N THE MORNING</small> of August 2nd, we were billeted at the Ferme de l'Espérance, resting for the first time since July 14th, apart from the two or three days when we were transported from the front in Champagne Pouilleuse at Auberive, to the front at Château-Thierry. Spending time at Espérance was not a pleasant prospect: we were too near that terrible Ourcq battlefield where we had suffered so much. So I welcomed my leave, and when the headquarters officers and the Colonel made their farewells I readily took their telegrams and promised to send them to Paris (by the way, this cost me quite a bit, and only Father Duffy thought of repaying me!).

The Colonel put his car at my disposal and after a number of breakdowns the little overworked Ford finally brought me to my destination, La Ferté. This was the only railway terminus still functioning. I drove through Château-Thierry at nightfall and took advantage of a flat tyre to have a stroll around the town. I was astonished to see the civilians back in their houses in great numbers. I had been just as surprised at Courpoil when I saw two or three old women returning only a few hours after the Germans had left, and when we were relieved on the 1st of August I noticed two women again, rummaging in the ruins of their houses at Villers-sur-Fère. This makes one wonder how these people could be liaising with the army: if there had been an officially organised repatriation programme, it could never have functioned at such a speed.

I joined my regiment at Goncourt. While I was away, the big event had been the formation of the 1st American Army, intended to win the St Mihiel salient for their début – as everybody knew. Whilst I was away the chaplain had celebrated a magnificent mass for the dead in the Forêt de Fère, and moved everybody to tears by the eloquence of his own memories of the dead. The chaplain was away when I returned. Having put all his energy into the battle he had finally succumbed to the effects of overwork. Above all he had suffered deep down in his heart. It had been a terrible, unbearable ordeal for him to bury these youths whom he knew, to search these swollen, hideous bodies whom he had loved when they were young and strong. One night Father Duffy came to our headquarters, very downcast, and there was envy in his words: he envied us because we were casual, we were active, and this stopped us thinking of the dead. His task was heavy, overwhelming and he had been taken ill, but before this he gave his sermon at the mass for the dead and, with Colonel McCoy, visited the grave of Quentin Roosevelt, pilot and son of the former American President, who had been buried by the Germans a few kilometres from the Forêt de Fère.

The 1st American Army was not often talked about but we were part of it. I found the staff headquarters of the Mission (the French delegation) with Commandant Corbabon billeted in Bourmont, a picturesque village set high on a hill and reached via a long, dusty, winding road. At the Mission I found Colonel McCoy. Corbabon told me that I had been nominated for various awards, the American DSC and my captain's stripes. I was happy and it did not occur to me that these hopes might never be fulfilled. McCoy was suntanned and had grown a moustache, which made him look old and tired. In fact I think he was very worried. All these actions which he had taken part in did not seem likely to bring him promotion or decoration; furthermore, he was in the Regular army. On July 1st, a long list of generals had been published with the names of many of his comrades: MacArthur was on it. They were Washington's promotions, politicians' promotions. As a Regular, McCoy had been nominated for the rank of brigadier by Pershing, with no result as yet. However, he did not have to wait long: before we left Bourmont he too was awarded the brigadier star and took command of the 32nd Infantry Division.

My arrival at Bourmont was not pleasant. I got there late, with the Colonel in his car. I awakened the American billeting major who gave me an address for my room. I got such a poor welcome from the landlady that I flew into a rage. She would have preferred to let her room to American soldiers, at a very high price, of course. Poor us! There was no excuse for her all-too-human weakness, and I should have remembered Marcus Aurelius' sad but true maxim, 'Be aware that today you are sure to meet a liar, a thief, a flatterer…' In spite of the woman I settled in, to the great amusement of the Americans, machine gunners woken by the altercation.

Sometime later we exchanged moving goodbyes with McCoy and treated him to a banquet, which the Americans thought was remarkable although the food was no more than nourishing, not high-quality. McCoy gave me an affectionate handshake. To my delight he said he sincerely hoped that I would receive the captain's stripes which I fully deserved, and assured me that they would not fail to come soon. Indeed he had taken care of this and it was thanks to him that Corbabon had nominated me. McKenna the womanizer had come back, barely affected by his brother's death and taking it lightly. Remarkably, McCoy did not even think of punishing this unprofessional officer who had been away during the action and put in only a short appearance during the last few days, and even then had stayed at the back.

I still recall how my faithful orderly, Avallet, a former Territorial from the Isère, had been teased by the Americans, who told him that I had been killed or seriously injured. This distressed the poor man and amused the Americans. I also remember how Patsy, as he was called by the Americans, had entrusted his friend Mougon with a bag containing my change of clothes, but how Mougon had lost it and forgotten all about it once he had arrived in the shelled area.

At Goncourt we stayed barely a few days. I remember soldiers parading along the Meuse, and some very hot days when the Americans went swimming naked in the river, without the slightest thought for people– men and women – walking past on the road. Here the Meuse is not very deep; it flows in a clay soil and is sometimes hemmed in by steep banks, like a small stream that cannot broaden its bed. We also spent about a week at Viocourt, where the manoeuvres started again, more intense than ever.

One day, amidst the dust, a demonstration attack was given by the Donovan Battalion using all infantry weapons, machine-guns, Stokes mortars and 37s. I had thought up this manoeuvre and I had no idea that our visitors would be the whole staff of the Division and even a few officers from Chaumont. Colonel Mitchell did not know this either: it was Donovan creating his own publicity. Because of this crowd, the manoeuvre was a bit of a failure and no use to anybody, with men packed together in spite of my repeated protests, advancing thoughtlessly with no attempts to liaise. The manoeuvre looked good but taught nothing. Honest, unselfish work is as rare in the French army as among the Americans, but as regards discipline it is such that a French major would not have taken the liberty to invite the Division staff to a parade without letting his Colonel know in advance.

Finally, the next billet, which left me with a lasting memory, was Bulligny near Toul. Every day we were advancing towards the St Mihiel front. I remember Bulligny because I did the billeting. I was outraged by the laziness of the officers who were sent to prepare our billets. At every stage it was the same story: three quarters of the men camped in tents, partly because there were no available premises, but above all through the fault of the billeting majors and our own billeting parties. At Bulligny I spent the whole afternoon and four or five hours of the night, waking up the inhabitants and getting them to find room for the Americans' arrival: I thought that we would be staying there for several days. About 1am there were only two units left to billet, and I showed the officer the last few houses where he could find them a shelter. But a moment later he confessed he had not found any room and decided his men should camp! Once again I was the one who had to wake up the last inhabitants so that I could place these two units. When the regiment arrived everybody had his bale of straw and his corner in an attic.

Those at the top thought it quite normal to allocate a 3000-strong regiment to a village with room for only two or three hundred (while the regiment in the neighbouring village had plenty of comfort and far too much space). Then the rest could camp out! And it was much easier for the billeting major and all the officers. In summer this could be forgiven; our men camped out at Viocourt. But with the September rains, leaving the men outside was ruining their health. And their health seemed precious to me in view of our coming attack; as far as I was concerned, bringing strong, rested, refreshed men to the line contributed to the success of the battle. But my efforts were to no avail. At the next stop I let the Americans manage on their own. As a consequence, all the men camped out in tents under a downpour and on a waterlogged site. This was at Toul or in its suburbs, in a region where there was all the room in the world to sleep in dry conditions!

At Bulligny, Mitchell was promoted colonel and I brought a bottle of Bulligny champagne to the mess to celebrate. Corbabon had been invited and it was a real feast. Father Duffy was back from Vittel. The next day, Pershing brought us the DSC awards for the most recent battles. To my astonishment I was not on the list, in spite of McCoy's and the brigadier general's promises. I was greatly disappointed, but I was not the only one: Chevalier too, Lawrence and Jacobson had been nominated for the DSC. All to no effect.

Finally the last stage from Toul put us in position behind our attacking front line. All these marches took place at night and with the greatest precautions. But inevitably, in spite of strict orders, when they arrived near the front, the Americans would become less cautious. Roads were cluttered with artillery convoys and columns of all sorts. As a result car drivers switched on their lights. To the Boche planes coming to reconnoitre the roads, it probably presented an extravaganza of intermittent lights. Headlights flashed on and off repeatedly: this was ridiculous. I had to argue with the Colonel who wanted to disregard the orders and switch on the headlights. I thought of all the human lives endangered by this lack of common sense. It was all to do with secrecy and the success of our attack. Americans did not have such scruples. Because of their frenzied individualism, they would not put up with the discipline that was necessary for their own safety.

On the other hand, ridiculous secrecy and laughable mistrust had surrounded all the preparations for the attack. On the pretext of keeping the secret until the last moment, the orders from the division arrived at Boucq the day before the attack and we did not have time to publish the regimental orders; the captains had even less time to write out their plan of attack. Fortunately the division had given us four copies, one for each battalion and one for the Colonel. Sectors were known only by hearsay, although I knew mine because the Colonel trusted me – I had almost become one of them since the battle of the Ourcq. But at Brigade Headquarters, my compatriot Mercier had to kick up a fuss and complain to the general in order to receive information of any kind. In fact, without knowing it, we French had become liaison officers, no longer instructors. I believe this change, which was never passed on to us by our Mission in Chaumont, was conceived and carried out by the Americans while the French knew nothing about it. Be that as it may, secret orders had been published about us, and McCoy had called me his Liaison Officer at the Ourcq, and earlier at Baccarat. I found this very surprising. At that time I was officially, for the French and for the Americans too, an instructing officer. Our title never changed, but the Americans had decided that they were tired of our interfering, which hurt their pride. We were kept in the dark. We were told too late about the orders to attack. We were not consulted any more.

After McCoy's departure, this attitude, which I sensed more than observed – even though I was privileged – upset me so much that all I could think of was leaving. After the battle at St Mihiel I complained bitterly to Meaney, now the second in command, about this ridiculous situation. In the regiment I did not even have the liaison assignments which justified Mercier's presence in the brigade. 'Oh!' replied Meaney amiably, 'you need not do any work. Your presence is all that matters. At least we know we are fighting the war more or less according to the rules.' I had become a regimental mascot!

Then followed those last days before the attack, with our troops stationed in the rain, in the mud, in the forest south of Seichefrey. Our headquarters was at Boucq but it was a very long way from us to the battalions and driving was hard on the muddy roads in the forest. In the daytime we were supposed to stay put, but the Germans were warned about the attack by the to-ing and fro-ing which was impossible to prevent. Staff cars alone would have been enough to inform the enemy and warn them of special preparations. The Boche 'sausage' (observation balloon) watched our rear mockingly and the observer up there could see the unloading of ammunition and sometimes would train his 150mm gun on to a dépôt and blow it up for fun.

I must admit I was worried. The Boche were quiet, but they could not have been ignorant of our movements. Even in the daytime, roads were cluttered with trucks, although only certain types of supplies had been authorised. In the woods, slippery and waterlogged lanes made overtaking the convoys impossible, and as the Americans had not regulated the flow of traffic, there were traffic holdups everywhere. In the daytime, this poor organisation had the obvious results. The roads were lined with trucks stuck in the mud, stranded at the edge or in the ditches. Our battalions had not positioned themselves accurately in the woods and on the first day it was very difficult to find them. In the Forêt de la Reine there was an indescribable mixture of units since none of them had gone to the place allocated by the Staff headquarters.

During these few days, from 9th to 15th, we were quite idle; the company officers did not reconnoitre the sector. The secret (and all its detail) had been so well kept that we knew nothing of the attack. However, those of us attached to the Colonel's staff were allowed to go on reconnaissance unofficially. On the 10th I visited our sector on my own; the trenches of the second line were full of water. My trouble was all for nothing as we were not to use the front or second lines. But I spotted a headquarters in which an artillery major had already set up. For the Colonel I had found a place almost on the ridge, between Beaumont and the Bois du Jury, north of the road.

I must admit that while the detailed arrangements of the attack were atrocious, the overall plan was excellent and bold . It had in fact been conceived by the French. Orders reached us during the day on the 11th. There was nothing we could do. A regimental order cannot be written a few hours before an attack. I remember how impatient I got about the Staff being so slow at every level. We had to get going somehow or other. We were aided by luck, the lack of morale and the inferior numbers of the Germans.

How tired I was during those September days! I had gone on reconnaissance with despair in my heart, and rather than walking I dragged my weary limbs. Bad food, irregular rest, disorganised American life had depressed and tired me out. I had lost my enthusiasm. The war seemed unending and infinitely sad. At Hamonville the civilians were leaving in view of the attack. In the same house as us was a woman who had just given birth, and she had to be taken away by car. Our poor country, our poor people! What a lot of suffering they had gone through! They were driven away by one army, then by the other, but still put on a brave face and endured their sufferings. Their resignation broke my heart, but I was still full of admiration.

The arrangements for the attack were as follows: Donovan's Battalion in the first wave would position themselves ahead of our line of resistance in an abandoned, overgrown area with an entanglement of old networks, where only our patrols ventured since the Germans had inflicted cruel losses on the Americans in a notorious raid. Placing a battalion in the open in this way and without shelter or trenches was daring, but the terrain was normally unoccupied and the enemy knew this. Moreover, our troops would only advance at the last minute and would stretch along the valley to the west of the Bois du Jury and to the east of Seicheprey, only one or two hours before dawn, when the attack was to start. Our objectives were marked by the following villages: St Boussans first (leaving Lehayville to our left), then Maizerais, Essey and Pannes. We had tanks with us and one detachment was responsible for filling in the trenches so that the tanks could go through. Indeed, as was not generally known, tanks (especially the small Renaults), could move over shell holes and narrow, strong trenches, but not the vast trenches and saps in the old defensive sectors. The tank is much more a weapon for a war of movement than for trench warfare. It requires billiard table smoothness and available shelter from artillery fire.

Our 2nd Battalion was very far behind the 1st, in front of, or level with Mandres aux Quatre Tours, the 3rd not very far behind. For once, the troops had been spread and ordered to keep their positions. The bloody attacks of the Chateau-Thierry days had at last served their purpose. The general plan was therefore excellent. It was audacious in that we were starting ahead of the line of the occupied trenches, yet cautious since the enemy could not foresee this. But the details were terrible. Nothing had been prepared because the regiment in charge had been informed too late. There were no depots for rifles, flares or grenades and no first aid posts. Troops were going up to the attack without the signals they needed to liaise. Some indeed, such as rockets, were non-existent in the lines. With regard to supplies, everyone did their best and at the last moment, an hour or less before our attacking line was set in motion, Donovan received what he needed. But what a night! It was terribly dark and it started to rain so that the ground became slippery and the men were soaked to the skin. The Colonel had gone up to his headquarters at nightfall. It was then a beautiful evening, which did not lead us to expect such a rainy night. Around our shelter, batteries had been set up in all the places already suitable, plus others in makeshift positions. That was promising! The brigade staff was in another shelter a bit further along the Beaumont road. The 166th Headquarters was at Beaumont and MacArthur of the 84th Brigade arrived and boldly took up a position on the ridge along the edge of the Bois du Jury, slightly ahead of us, to watch events.

Night came, horribly gloomy and the rain soon drenched the ground. Our troops were coming up with difficulty, I could tell. Peering into the darkness I pictured the slow march of the columns, the fits and starts and the long halts. Also I had a foreboding that our flare supplies would never arrive on time. But I was mistaken. The Americans had to expend much more physical energy than the French to obtain the same result, because they had no foresight, no plans, no methods, no organisation. When they achieved success – dearly paid for – this was always a mystery to me. Whenever I read the short, incomplete orders from their staff officers, my face fell and I was unable to conceal my resentment on seeing such unsatisfactory preparations. Merle-Smith and Mitchell were amused when I told them I never understood how they could be so lucky. 'Nothing works, yet we are always OK!' In fact, examining these events more closely solves the enigma for me. The Americans always received considerable help from the French, if only from their artillery support, which we got a lot of till the end, including the days of the Meuse battle – that most American of battles. The Germans were losing their stranglehold at last. Their defeat was patently obvious and we could allow ourselves many errors, many faults that would have cost thousands of lives in 1917. In Montfaucon in October I saw the whole infantry of the 42nd massed together in the forest on an area of a few hectares, six or seven kilometres away from the enemy guns.

In those ravaged, jagged woods where we camped in shell holes, thousands of fires were burning; our men sat by them and warmed themselves – their only comfort. Not a single shell ever came to trouble our peace, in spite of the German aircraft flying above us. The Germans had more to think about than harming us in the rear. The Americans entered the war when the enemy was getting weaker and had already lost its aggressive spirit.

In short, the St Mihiel offensive had plainly been planned with a view to enhancing the reputation of the American army, its whole design assuring it of success. At a time when the enemy was under attack from all sides and had nowhere else to post reserves, this one little salient was a weak spot, soon to be evacuated by the Germans in any case: they would abandon it without resistance.

The day of the battle dawned, the 12th September, and our troops were in position. The enemy still made no move although they were showing signs of life and for the past few days had fired a few cannon rounds over the main road behind the command post. They were obviously aware of the coming danger. What I do not understand is why, forewarned as they were, they did not evacuate the salient before the attack. Judging by the fact that we only took 1600 prisoners, there must have been very few men in the trenches. There was a minimum of artillery and evacuating the salient would have been a simple matter, considering the small number of troops deployed there. The inhabitants of Pannes had assured us on the evening of the 12th and again on the 13th that the Germans knew of the planned attack. On the 12th all the civilians had received the order to take to their cellars and shelters and the Germans began to withdraw. In spite of all this, they showed a kind of lackadaisical short-sightedness that still surprises me. It was not possible for just a few thousand men to hold out and they were in fact being sacrificed. The German high command, knowing there was no way they could resist, was too proud to give up the game even when it was lost. And the salient of St Mihiel proved to be easy prey, a success of which we had been certain.

We opened fire at the appointed time. The sky was alight with the ceaseless crisscrossing of our shells. From the German side a few white flares seemed to be defying us. It was the battle of Champagne all over again but this time with only one side attacking. Like us then, although they had not carried out a raid, the Germans had been miraculously alerted and they knew the exact date and hour of our infantry attack. The battle of St Mihiel was probably for us what the advance on Château Thierry and Amiens had been for the Germans..

By first light our troops were advancing. I made my way to the top of the hill and witnessed the glorious, unforgettable sight of wave after wave of Americans sweeping over the Plaine de Woevre. In the distance, to the left, I could make out with my field-glasses the lines moving forward as if on a parade ground. St Baussant and Mazerais in front of us must surely have been taken. Our shells hammered into the ground and produced a dense protective curtain ahead of the advance. The dark outline of the terrifying hill of Mont-sec was covered time and again with swirls of blue smoke from the explosions. This epic scene brought to mind (though in a smaller way), the heroic victory of 24th October 1916, the advance of De Salins and Passaga Divisions, which I had witnessed from the heights of Fumin Wood where I had been in a support unit behind the 74th.

Yet how different this was! This was an easy victory without losses, even without prisoners, it seemed. The enemy artillery was almost silent and there was not the slightest sound of a machine gun. In 1916, except on the left flank where the preparations had been more careful, the 74th had suffered bloody losses in front of Fort de Vaux. From 7a.m. onwards the machine guns had rattled out and halted the 291st and the Chasseurs. We had been crushed under a formidable barrage, through which I crossed with my unit with great difficulty and great loss of life. But the battle of St Mihiel unfolded without a hitch. It is not surprising that the Americans sometimes thought themselves superior to us after this battle of St Mihiel, which was little more than a military stroll. It had been perfectly designed to go to the heads of beginners.

Minutes later I was taking leave of the Colonel to go off to reconnoitre a command post in the conquered territory. There were still no prisoners. It was as if we had entered a desert. It was not until we got up to Maizerais that Donovan took his first prisoners in the shelters hollowed out in Hill 235. Before that, up at St Boussant, I discovered a German Mauser emplacement with traces of recent occupation. The second Mauser was on the parapet, but there were no empty cartridges and the belts were intact. Not a shot had been fired although our first abandoned lines were well within the line of fire. The gunners' equipment lay higgledy-piggledy in the shelter where there was straw, or rather freshly-cut hay, on the bunks. The food supplies were there, ready for the return of the sentries. Around the emplacement, no sign of shell holes. These men had fled without a fight and yet what a fine mission they could have accomplished! What a role they would have filled! The courage of a handful of Germans would have cost the lives of hundreds of Americans. At

Boussaint I caught sight of Chevalier from the Mission, who was accompanying the tanks. Poor tank regiment! They were not needed here. A few shells fell on the heights of St Boussaint. The rattle of a distant machine-gun could be heard. While I was talking to Chevalier the troops of Anderson Battalion passed by under sporadic shellfire, without any losses, as if on parade. Soon we were eating the provisions left by the Germans, butter, honey, or rather substitutes, some good tinned stuff. What more could one wish for? And I hadn't eaten for 72 hours. However, eating the disgusting bread didn't agree with me and I paid for my hunger with horrible stomach pains.

Further on, I stopped again at an abandoned artillery command post. Very close by there was a deserted emplacement, which our shells had shattered unnecessarily, as it had long since been left empty. My impression was that in these quiet sections the Germans had reduced the garrisons to a minimum some time ago. There was little artillery or infantry and both were of mediocre quality. In front of us we had Poles. Further to the left, the French found Austrians. In fact it seems not to have been true that the German forces of early 1918 had been hugely swelled by defectors. To judge by our St Mihiel attack, the German defensive front was extremely weak and the numbers deployed there even more reduced than ours. Everywhere were trenches of all kinds, abandoned long ago, and concrete emplacements dating back to 1915, which had not been used for months. I had promised to show the Americans a powerful trench system, fantastic shelters and a highly-developed defence strategy, but all was abandoned and ruined.

I recall stopping for a long time at this second shelter. I found everything I needed for my toilet and outside in the bright sunshine I performed my ablutions and shaved with delight. I waited for the Colonel who had told me which road he was coming by, but he did not appear until nightfall. The German artillery had gone quiet. A bright sun shone over the terrain, scarcely been touched by the war during the last 24 hours. Compare this with the devastation of 1915! A few fresh shell-holes here and there were scarcely noticeable in ground which still bore the raw scars of 1915. Our shelling had successfully put the Germans to flight, but three or four hours preparatory firing, even heavy, causes little damage when the shells are travelling many kilometres.

I remember very well that this artillery shelter was delightful. One could imagine a German soldier who had dreamt of finishing the war there in comfortable safety, fed by hope. Men have few needs, when it comes down to it, and conscious that he could have been much worse off, this man found deep satisfaction in the dull, wretched life of a calm front. What pleasure is to be found in these little 'homes from home' after the sleepless weariness of the front line! A good book, a wire-mesh bed at the bottom of a trench, water for washing, comrades to share a laugh with and a feeling of being surrounded by human friendship, that is all that kept thousands of men patient, all they aimed for and dreamt of in the lines. The smallest pleasure becomes delightful when one is putting up with huge numbers of privations. Nothing leads us to gentle, melancholy dreaming more than the periods of respite between dangers. We are moved even by rays of sunshine. The smallest scrap of life becomes precious – a butterfly, a bird, a lark high in the sky. A wild flower captures our imagination. We are like the prisoner who discovers a spindly stalk, sown by the wind, shooting up between the paving slabs.

At Verdun, perhaps what had filled the soul with terror was the complete absence of life – death, death, everywhere. The very tree roots no longer grew. It was with indescribable joy one morning that I had found a slender, leafy stem on the trunk of a dead tree in front of the Batterie de l'Hopital. Just for a moment, here at Maizerais I gave way to this melancholy dreaming. As I walked I saw a few vines which were still recognisable. One day life would return to its former activity. These ruins at Maizerais would be rebuilt and the war would be forgotten. It would gradually disappear into the past, vanishing like some terrifying meteor, and the little quarrels of men would begin again. This village would rise again from its ruins, immediately returning, or trying to return to its former self. Mankind would not change. The only traces left by this huge suffering would be a desperate search for deeper forgetfulness through ever more intense pleasures.

Spencer, who was accompanying me, took a German bicycle and went on to Pannes. As for me, I waited impatiently for the Colonel for a few more hours. All was calm, not the least sign of shells. The salient had at this stage been completely captured and there were no more Germans at St Mihiel. Eventually, as Mitchell did not turn up, I set off again and soon arrived at Essey. That poor village! Those poor people!

I noticed civilians before seeing any German prisoners at all. No doubt they had been sent a different way. In fact, in spite of Donovan's exaggerations, the number of prisoners did not exceed 50 to 100 as far as I could make out. For the whole division the numbers amounted to about 300. In front of us, the enemy had good roads along which to beat their retreat. Unlike the troops on the salient itself, they would not be exposed to the danger of being cut off. In fact, if we had pushed forward from the first day as far as St Benoit, we would have captured many thousands of Germans, since St Benoit and Beney were important junctions. It was here that the roads from the west converged with those coming south from the salient.

When I arrived at Essay, I would never have believed that there could still be any remaining civilians. What I discovered were the wretched ruins of a village that had been under ceaseless bombardment since 1914. Houses had been demolished and left in ruins, their roofs caved in, after the Boche had removed material in order to construct their shelters. At the centre of the village it was with great surprise that I spotted a woman's face at a window, gaunt and sallow with suffering. Of course, the people welcomed me with a show of friendliness, but there was no enthusiasm. Poor things! They were depressed and unable to make an effort. They looked demoralised and completely worn out. For my part, I could not help being a little suspicious. How had they dared to remain in this destroyed village? How had they survived the multiple shellings that had brought the houses down over their heads? They were living in the ruins of a house where the cement-reinforced roof provided a shell-proof blockhouse.

"A Frenchman!" shouted the sickly-looking woman, who asked me in so she could explain that they had stayed against their will.

"The Germans forced us to stay. We kept a small cow and gave them our milk. And then, I suppose, we helped them escape some of the surprise shelling. The Germans forced us to stay because they knew the French would think twice before firing on a village which was still inhabited."

It appears that even in Maizerais, where there wasn't a stone left standing, an old woman had persisted in staying. Perhaps she was still there. I could scarcely believe this, having myself walked through ruins already overgrown with grass, and seen the jumbled heaps of stone which marked where the houses had been. It is nevertheless a fact that French civilians everywhere would have stayed in their villages at the front if we had not evacuated them. In Lorraine, in the Baccarat sector, the village of Migainville served as headquarters for a battalion only 2km from the front, yet there were still about twenty inhabitants here. In all the houses were people who had escaped. In the very jaws of the fighting, in zones occupied by the enemy, some of these good folk still went out to gather the willow twigs on which their livelihood depended.

The unthinking bravery of civilians has always struck me. In 1917, when the communiqués were full of the shelling of Rheims, one day I visited this great town and its cathedral. It is a day which will live forever in my memory. This sublime jewel of French Gothic art still retained its divine beauty, in spite of its injuries. Its slender grace, the soaring columns, were astonishing when one considered how the building had stood up to attack, and how limited was the damage it had suffered from the 350s. What power, what centuries-old architecture is in these vaults, untouched by our puny weapons! The holes made by the heavy Austrian shells only emphasised the contrast between the hidden strength of the building and the pure, graceful beauty of its slender lines. In the radiant July sunshine the least damaged façade seemed to reach up and lose itself in the heavens for which it was meant.

But what was my astonishment when I caught sight of a good woman hurrying across the square, basket on her arm, no doubt on her way to the market! All the inhabitants of Reims, as I later confirmed, imagined that while their houses remained unscathed, the enemy artillery could not hit them. Some had even found mathematical reasons, for example in the lie of the land, to justify their confidence and thus slept soundly in their beds. Wasn't it in the Ardennes villages, after all, where children used to wander about amidst shell and bullet fire and where the inhabitants proudly showed me their roofs smashed by shells?

"We were all round the fire," a good woman said to me, referring no doubt to their most recent escape, "when the first shell knocked down the chimney, which tumbled into the hearth and put the fire out".

"Come and see my bomb-proof cellar," said the Mayor. "It has been well-tested. We got a direct hit from a 150." And he showed me a vaulted cellar where a sinister-looking crack and some loose rubble showed that a second shell would easily have broken through, almost into their shelter. I think, then, that these civilians on the salient had willingly played along with the enemy. But spending four years in a village raked by shellfire every day, in these dangerous ruins, spending these four years with the Germans, working and slaving for them and what's more, protecting them, that I will never understand and it still astonishes me. The love of country people for their land must truly be stronger than their love of life.

But I did not stop long at Essey. I had already delayed too long. I wanted to re-join Donovan, since the Colonel had not come. Essey was not far from Pannes and I set out straight away. It was just outside Pannes that the vanguard had to stop for the night. Essey had scarcely been touched by our shells, or rather the damage in the middle of the ruins was scarcely visible, apart from some extra bits of rubble thrown out on to the road. At Pannes and on the Pannes-Essey road, the damage inflicted by our artillery was more apparent, and also further along, especially beyond Pannes. The trees on the Essey road were broken and shattered by the storm of our shells. The road followed by the retreating Germans could not have been very pleasant. Here and there the route was marked by German bodies and dead horses. At Pannes even whole teams of horses had been massacred by our shells on the Pont de la Madine. The enemy had beaten a hasty retreat, leaving stores full of clothing and provisions of all sorts.

The Americans had not been more than an hour in the town before one could spot the ones who had kitted themselves out in German boots taken from the shoe-store. Others were wearing German greatcoats picked up on the battlefield. The nights were cold and the Americans had not been issued with their greatcoats, having only one blanket and their slicker (waterproof). A few of them, men from the 167th and the 165th, were already drunk. There was an officers' mess ('Kasino') with an abundance of alcohol, including excellent Rhine wines, German champagne, and a 'Soldatenheim' (soldiers' canteen) full of bottles of pink lemonade. The beer flowed and as they passed, men stopped at the side of the road where tapped barrels had been placed and filled their canteens or the big tin mugs which fitted on them.

It was in Pannes rather than Essey where I became aware of the moral havoc wreaked by the German occupation. Here, the civilians were really pitiful in the way they were still dominated by the spectre of the Germans, even as they retreated, beaten. The most sensible, mature men would still drivel on:

"Well, they did say to us, 'Take care! It will mean certain death for you when we go,'" said a fellow of about fifty who looked like a gamekeeper. And when a few wounded Germans went past in the street, he began to tremble and lost his head.

"Oh! Now we're done for! The Americans have attacked them. They will be back to flatten the village with their shells!"

I have never seen people so terrified as these poor villagers. They shouted in indignation about the delay in evacuating civilians. They expected the German revenge at any moment. What evil enemies these Germans were to have left such an impression, such strong fear in people's minds even after they had taken to their heels. The words of the gamekeeper, reminding them of the threats of the enemy (however impossible to carry out) counted for more than all my protestations. They took no account of us and it was in vain that I tried my best to reassure them.

The Germans did not seem to be carrying out their threats, at least for the next few days, and so I spent a peaceful night in Pannes. The poor woman who put me up decided to cook us a rabbit and it was thanks to me that the Colonel, who arrived very late in the evening, was able to eat something and rest. I also found a bed for Father Duffy.

The headquarters had been set up in the old German command post right in the centre of the village, near the main road. We spent a good part of the night in idle chitchat. The Americans are very good at long, useless discussions. You waste your time completely, not even talking about the fighting. I would have a job to tell you what we did discuss. And so, on that evening, I never heard any orders concerning the next day's action. And to think that the Americans are supposed to be men of action who look down on us French because we hesitate so long! In reality we are the ones who know how to act, and it is the Americans who are always taken by surprise with nothing prepared. That night I began to think they would not bother with dinner; I really felt like sitting down at the table by myself. Captain Merle-Smith kept us up more than half the night, to no purpose. In the end, I managed to persuade them to get some rest. I took Father Duffy to some good folks who put everything at our disposal in the way of food and bedding.

The rest of the night could not have been more peaceful. How good-hearted these French women are! They showed such generosity in providing us with all their poor households had to offer. But the Americans were soon to forget this. They took for granted the homage of these poor victims of the war and were much more grateful to the Germans for their generosity in defeat after the occupation. Any American officer deemed by his fellows to be 'worth his salt' expended his energy and willingly sacrificed himself, needlessly facing all possible dangers at the front. On being given orders, the manner in which he carried them out mattered not at all, provided that the officer was seen to be sacrificing all his comforts, neither sleeping nor eating. In other words, being a good American soldier, whether in the ranks or at officer level, meant above all being able to tolerate any manner of unnecessary difficulties. The ideal colonel would die of hunger and sleep on the ground while his liaison officers lounged in bed. He would sleep two hours a night, eat only poor food at irregular intervals and waste his time on futile matters, overlooking what was important, forgetting the elementary rule of foresight.

In short, an American command was a mess of useless strain and effort, out of all proportion with the results. And sometimes, unfortunately, the orders drawn up were of such criminal ignorance that countless lives were needlessly lost. Our allies really knew how to do things when they put their minds to it! The entire September offensive should furnish ample proof: thousands of Americans perished, victims of the unbelievable stupidity of their superiors. Moreover, the divisional commanding officers behaved in exactly the same way as those in my regiment. They bivouacked under canvas when there was no reason to do so. And it was not as if they were always very near to the front (I have never known a French commanding officer stay so cautiously behind the lines). They used their huge tents, setting them up on muddy ground where everyone got bogged down. At Ferte-sous-Jarre I saw a divisional commanding officer collapsing with weakness because he had not eaten or slept for forty-eight hours. And indeed, he was proud of himself, whilst I despised such idiotic behaviour.

All this carelessness, this absence of method, this lack of foresight made me furious. The Americans did not have the art of living. Even so, they frequently reproached us for what they called our petty economising. According to them, we were mean spirited, we did not think big, we were not daring enough, and we fussed over details which would not have concerned them. Of course, we were less free-and-easy than they were, and not as bold, but that was because we thought before we acted. For me, life at an American headquarters was hellish: less for the privations we endured there, than for the pointlessness of these privations and the humiliating stupidity of the chaos.

The next day, September 13th, Father Duffy and I helped with the evacuation of the poor people, nearly all of whom had spent the night in shelters under the church. Soon American ambulances came to take them away. These unfortunate villagers were only allowed small parcels of belongings. Among them an old Frenchman especially filled me with pity. He was on a stretcher, dying, his distraught daughter by his side. An American soldier had shot and wounded the old man, mistaking him for a German in the darkness of the shelter where the civilians had been herded by the German officials since the evening of the 11th of September.

The next day our troops advanced along the southern edge of the Bois de Thiancourt, as far as the farm at Hassavant, to the north of St. Benoît, without encountering the enemy. We had made a grave error, or rather the staff officers had, by not taking, on the first night and in one action, the crossroads I mentioned earlier. Throughout the night the flow of troops coming from St. Mihiel or the Hauts de Meuse streamed quietly by, one kilometre from our outposts. MacArthur, a brave and energetic man, full of daring, was partly responsible for this setback. He had attacked and, together with his French staff officer, his second-in-command, Captain X, and his interpreter, had spent the whole day at the front, 100 metres from the creeping barrage. MacArthur was well aware of the fatigue his men were suffering, and of their need for rest and fresh supplies, and so that night he refused to continue with the advance. We were the nearest troops; another five kilometres and we could have taken St. Benoît, which would not have been any more difficult to take than Pannes had been. We would have cut off the retreat of several thousand fugitives, their guns and entire supply trains. Later, in the forest, I noticed obvious signs of the great haste of the German retreat. The road coming from the Hauts de Meuse crosses the Forêt de Vigneulles on the way to St. Benoît, and was the only escape route for the garrisons of the Hauts de Meuse and St. Mihiel. All around abandoned rifles and other equipment were left behind. Vehicles had been overturned in ditches and abandoned. But the enemy had fallen back without incident and we advanced on our second objective on the 13th of September without taking a single prisoner. There had hardly been any contact with the enemy until the 84th Brigade spotted them at Haumont; and we met them in the Bois de la Grande Souche.

On the 13th September I took the gently sloping tree-lined road which connects Pannes to Beney, then turns at a right angle to go on to St. Benoît. At Pannes I witnessed the column of evacuees from Beney. Here, a poor old woman who still had not lost her sense of mischief despite the hardships she had suffered, shamelessly informed me that not all the babies in this caravan of people were French, "Far from it! Alas!" In the midst of a huge disaster, there is always some consolation, and this old woman found it in a bit of gossip.

I went on through Beney without stopping. The Americans of the 89th were already established there, having taken possession of all the houses left empty after the departure of the civilians. The second battalion of our regiment had come to a halt to the north of the Bois de Beney. The leading companies were positioned level with the Ferme de Sébastopol, and it was here that Major Anderson established his command post. A good French woman, fleeing as soon as they arrived, had handed over the farm and all her possessions, including a well-stocked farmyard and one or two cows in the shed. The Anderson battalion had had a bean-feast for a good part of the day. The men were starving, so in no time at all, rabbits were killed, skinned and roasted. During all this time when our food supplies were not getting through, many men survived on potatoes and on supplies taken from German depots, or even on cabbages picked from gardens and eaten raw. A few days later, we were relieved by the 84th Brigade, and fell back to Lamarche. Here I witnessed the stripping bare of what remained of a cabbage field by a battalion of voracious locusts – the Yanks. For a while a rumour went round that the field had been contaminated with mustard gas from our shells and that it was dangerous to eat the greens, but it made no difference.

At St. Benoît the Germans had burned down the church and some of the houses. The beautiful stately chateau, the stark outline of which stood out proudly above the village, was also burning away. Our soldiers and those of the other brigade arrived and extinguished the blaze, which had only reached one wing. The town of St. Benoît had served as a hideout for the German staff headquarters, and no doubt it was thanks to the presence of these important individuals that most of the village was set on fire. I did not realise immediately that there were still locals here, and I saw only a few individuals. There was not much time to question them. The civilians in Beney had warned us that the chateau was mined but our first act was to go up and establish a base there. MacArthur did the same. As for Lenihan, he came to visit us there after the 13th, but his experiences of the château de la Forêt still being fresh in his mind, he soon gave up coming so close to the front. The château was on the line of resistance, and our outposts, barely one kilometre away, were in a straight line from the ridge of la Grande Souche. On the 13th and the days following, the enemy had fun burning the village of Haumont, which they believed we held. We would see a German run out of a house which a few moments later went up in flames. The Kriemhilde Stellung, undeniably a formidable defence system, passed immediately behind the village, parallel with the road to Woel.

German trenches in this retreat position were almost non-existent. The Germans were working feverishly on the networks and shelters. We watched them throughout the day as, right under our noses, they swarmed about the trenches trying to reinforce them. They soon re-took Haumont, where MacArthur did not want to risk his men. During all this time the German artillery was keeping very quiet. However, a few shells were dropped on the château on the 13th. That was not surprising with all these men milling about in the parks and gardens! Housed in the cellars were a number of men from the 165th, the 167th, the liaison of the Colonel and the Brigadier-General. The chateau was not greatly damaged. The Germans had been preparing to move out and had assembled some furniture, pictures and mirrors in the interior courtyard. However, they had not had time to take them away. They had chosen badly! In their haste (or was it a touch of conscience?) they left behind a magnificent gold chalice, presented to the church by the owners of the chateau. I had never seen objects chosen with so little taste: vases, paintings, furniture and rather ordinary modern mirrors, which were in my opinion garishly ornate and vulgar. This task had obviously been done by rank-and-file soldiers – their officers were the first to take flight.

From the chateau one could see the German lines in the distance, and to the north the whole of the Woëvre plain spread out. What a gloriously beautiful sight! The country of France lay almost within our grasp. Here we came to a stand-still, facing an imagined line of resistance that a few tanks and some shelling could have quickly overcome. Obviously the French commanders did not intend continuing this attack, nor would they take full advantage of its success. We had taken possession of the salient without encountering any resistance and by the attack on St. Mihiel we had achieved an easy victory for the American Generalissimo; that was the important factor. The St Mihiel offensive had fulfilled its role.

Just as Laplace[10] had discovered his planet, I was the one who discovered the observation post on the chateau, simply by glancing at the map: all it took was a simple calculation of the contour lines. The top of the chateau overlooked the gently rolling countryside to the North. We occupied the chateau for a few days, which Donovan spent on the outpost at Hassavant Farm. I established contact with the French, and I recall the long hike to them through Vigneulle Forest. I followed a tangle of winding paths through the woods, large swathes of which the Germans had cut down in their usual manner. The commander, a captain in this case, was in a clearing on the crest of a hill well to our left. From those few days at the chateau at St. Benoît I recall the following incidents:

The first one I offer as a good example of the lack of initiative so characteristic of the Americans. Even though I was still unaware of the position of Donovan's or Anderson's battalions (we were never told anything), when we climbed up to St. Benoît on the 13th with Colonel Mitchell, we came upon a battalion on the right of the road, 500 metres south of the village. It was an extraordinary sight. Not only were they in an exposed position (they could have sheltered from view in the trees), but also they were drawn up loosely against artillery fire. The battalion, still in square formation, were busy digging trenches. The result? Lines of men, one behind the other, were positioned perpendicular to the front. The poor chaps had not even thought of changing their plan of action with a view to forward movement, nor altering their defensive lines to properly establish their position. I was ashamed and embarrassed at first, thinking that this was one of our battalions, and I advised the Colonel to get this absurd error corrected. However, it concerned the 167th Alabama Regiment, and therefore nothing to do with me. From the chateau of St. Benoît I could make out another battalion from the same regiment, 500 metres to the north. Here was the front line battalion in the same formation. They were digging themselves in deeper and deeper, so entrenched that they were unable to fire their rifles, lined up behind each other as they were. Commander Corbabon could not believe his eyes!

Another incident, more amusing this time, concerned a short journey I made by car on the 14th of September with Jacobson from the artillery unit. Our outposts were at Hassavant, but on our way to Woël we did not know if the French had reached them or if the Boche were between us and Woël, blocking and occupying the road. Jacobson picked me up and we set off, but without our driver whom Jacobson had led to believe that the roads were mined. Halfway to Woël, after passing the Donovan outposts, we came upon Legros, the interpreter, who was retracing his steps. He was in charge of evacuating civilians from Woël, but a French patrol had dissuaded him from going any further. For a short time we had the impression, as we sped towards Woël, that at any minute we might be stopped by machine gun fire coming from the trees lining the road – a most unpleasant experience. Quietly, I got my revolver ready. I think only Jacobson was enjoying it. Fortunately, the Boche had abandoned the road, for Woël had been taken. We met cavalrymen on foot. There had been no civilians in Woël for a few hours. Unfortunately,

French artillery had killed a French woman during the action. The German attack started after the cavalry arrived, however, during our visit it was very quiet. Only an observation balloon in the distance bothered us a little, and the cavalry men advised us to be careful. Jacobson searched through various shelters and houses including the curé's house, looking for souvenirs. Roadside ditches, shelters and rooms were full of scattered debris: dressings, rifles, bullets, grenades. In the centre of the village the bodies of some dead Austrians were beginning to make the air stink. Eventually we came across a room which had been used as a warehouse and from here we took possession of various pieces of equipment, including saddles, harnesses and the like. That is how I came to acquire an Austrian saddle. Those poor Austrians had brought with them enormous chests full of maps – Italian maps. They had not even been able to get rid of them before leaving for France.

There is a kind of attraction in running risks and looking for adventures. All the same, that expedition was less exciting at the time than it seems now. Other memories come back to me, hours both happy and sad in Dampvitoux Forest which is to the right of Hassavant Farm. I had made the correct decision not to take my horse, for several were killed when the chateau was shelled, so I explored the forest on foot, searching out German camps marked on the map. Most had been burned down, like those in the forest of Vigneulles. I recall my visits to Donovan in his headquarters at the farm, where he had taken over some very comfortable German hospital huts. He was always friendly. I fail to see what he could have done if the Boche had launched a counter-attack. No one had prepared any defence plan and not one trench had been dug. The battalion was comfortably housed in all these huts, and mobile field kitchens were set up at the farm. The enemy was content to bombard them for one night with a few 150s, which overshot the target. What terror it caused! Just imagine: it would have been complete panic if the Germans had merely attempted a small raid, let alone attacked in force.

At the rear, no one was patrolling the forest of Dampvitoux. The 3rd Battalion were based some distance away on one flank of the French. They were guarding nothing: the enemy could have come through, in force, between them and us, thus cutting the battalion off from the line. But the Boche never suspected there was a battalion in this precarious and risky position. Our enemy simply went on digging their trenches feverishly, waiting for the attack to start. It cannot be denied that Donovan took great pride in this ridiculous position even though he was exposing the whole battalion to capture or to being crushed by enemy artillery fire. Between Hassavant Farm and the southern edge of the Bois de la Souche, were two kilometres where the enemy could infiltrate. In the end the French filled the gap with small machine gun posts. But Donovan was happy with his position, separated from us as he was, without this having any tactical significance. It was enough for him to chase adventure and to put himself in danger. I complained loudly about this, but in the end all I got were some permanent patrols at the corner of the wood, bordering the road to the Farm on the west, and Bayern Strasse (Haumont Road) to the south. I was the only one talking sense. Americans have no idea of the principles of clear reasoning and logic. I was coming up against stubborn and incredulous people. It was very fortunate that the Germans were a spent force at this time, or we might have witnessed some dreadful disasters.

One day, coming from Hassavant Farm, I attended the burial of a French soldier on the edge of the wood. He had been killed by a shell whilst patrolling the American sector. Poor young man, buried without a prayer and without ceremony! I felt duty-bound to record his name and to take his papers: he was a poor youth of Class 16[11]. How sad war is! I thought of his parents, his friends, of those who would be waiting for him. Their distress, their sadness would be more intense, more unbearable if they knew he had been buried like this, by strangers, with no priest, no funeral service. The Americans did what they could, and the young soldier was laid in his grave without a coffin. He lay beside German coffins – each one more imposing than the other, extolling courage, patriotism, the virtues of those who lay there, the dead from the German hospital. In death there are no enemies; the body dressed in sky blue lay beside those in grey greatcoats.

I forgot to mention the defensive line in front of the chateau, including the ridiculous positions taken by the machine guns, all placed so that they had no field of fire. Lord above, how absurd! Fortunately the engineers arrived with a working plan – but then only on the last day. For at least four days no one from the infantry wanted to dig at all. Orders had arrived announcing that the engineers were in charge of setting up the line of resistance. I really would like to have seen the Americans during the earlier years of the war, or in those critical situations of the retreat in open country at the beginning of 1918. There would have been little remaining of this division after 24 hours, despite the so-called guts of the Americans. The German prison camps would have been filling up rapidly. I had never come up against such incompetence, laziness, such general disorder: as long as all was going well, what was the use of planning? If the Germans were not shooting, it was too early to dig holes, to take defensive measures in case they attacked or shelled us! I know of no other people who valued intellectual inertia as highly as the Americans. We need not envy their resistance to thinking! I still wonder anxiously what would have become of those masses of people gathered round the chateau if the enemy had been just a little nastier, more aggressive: a great many wasted lives! But luck was on our side.

Around the 16th September the 84th Brigade relieved us and took over our sector. We, the 165th, were the attacking regiment par excellence in the division. In our brigade I sought in vain for an example of where the 166th Regiment had acted boldly. Was it perhaps at Villers-sur-Fère, where, 24 hours too late, its battalions advanced on Seringes and Nesles? Or perhaps even at St. Mihiel where, unlike us, the 166th remained cautiously in reserve, when they could have been level with us. At least this saved some lives, and it was fortunate for those long-suffering soldiers from Ohio, led by Haugh – a wealthy and influential landowner – and not much of a colonel[12]. Outside Landres-Saint-Georges in the Meuse, Brigadier General Lenihan, and Mitchell, my Colonel, were suspended from duties by Summerall; but Haugh, whose headquarters was four kilometres behind ours, and his outposts one kilometre behind, escaped censure, protected by politicians. All praise to the democratic Army of the 49 States, and the legendary honesty of Washington's descendants!

At last, around the 17th September, we were relieved by the 84th Brigade who took over our entire sector. Our regiment went on leave as close to the front as possible, as was customary in the American army. The regimental command post, together with the first-aid station, was at Lamarche. We were billeted on a huge farm there, which more or less made up the whole village. The staff headquarters of the 166th was very close by, and sometimes I went to visit Lawrence there. I set up my own headquarters in a small well-furnished hut where I had a fire, a comfortable bunk, and peace. The more the Americans gained in confidence, the more I became a spare part in the regiment. And so, although demoralised, I took each day as it came. These memories of Lamarche are mingled with sadness and joy: especially the sadness at having to live in those vile barracks swimming in mud. The only access to my little wooden hut was through a stinking farmyard, complete with muddy puddles. Sadness also because my allotted role was diminishing. To cap it all I fell ill: an abscess on my wrist troubled me for some days. Above all, I felt sorry for the soldiers squelching about in the woods. I protested against the incompetence that had led to them camping when there were enough German huts in the forest to house them all. My protestations were completely futile. I became disheartened and did not even bother to visit the camps, because I was bound to return demoralised, sure that my attempts at changing the situation would be pointless.

Alongside these periods of mental depression and physical suffering, I had moments of happiness – that glimmer of happiness which can still shine in the war, refusing to be dimmed, though little light is left. I recall short strolls about the village, along hedges covered in berries and blossom: redcurrants, hawthorn, sloes, pale white clusters of flowers on the wild vines. German kitchen gardens brought a touch of brightness to the countryside, comforting because they spoke of the possibility of peace returning, and of honest fruitful labour. I would visit Mercier at Brigade Headquarters, either on the way to, or returning from Pannes. He and the general were billeted in charming forest huts, where German staff officers had been very comfortably housed earlier. Perhaps some people will say that the taste of that enemy of ours was unrefined, but that was not my impression. In time of war the least attempt at making one's surroundings more attractive is to be praised, even if it is only partly successful. In any case, the Germans succeeded in building forest huts which I found pleasing, in keeping with the countryside, and above all completely camouflaged. Inside, the rooms were light and cheerful, decorated with carved or painted panelling, or papered, or had brightly coloured curtains. They had verandas where you could be outside, yet sheltered from the rain. While the exterior of these outwardly rustic houses was ornamented with moss and bark, the interiors were very modern and luxurious.

By contrast, in Pannes, it was chaos, American-style. Untethered mules wandered about with no one to look after them, or they crowded together, scratching themselves, kicking out, wallowing in the mud. Close by, the sight of dead animals spoke volumes about the lack of care afforded them by the American support units. There were groups of men, some strolling about, some in shirts or half-naked sitting round the fires de-lousing their clothes. They were crammed into the small gully just outside the village, out in the open, their tents pitched nearby without the least camouflage. There was a waste of oats, hay, provisions, tinned food, which the Americans found easy to ignore. Here, a heap of good hay was rotting in the mud; over there, kit, equipment, and rusty rifles lay abandoned in a shell-hole. Cartridge belts or bandoliers trailed everywhere – battle debris that these masses of idle men could easily have picked up and put into piles. This was wastage that the French would not have contemplated, even at the start of the war and in the most tragic of circumstances.

We relieved the 168th (the Iowans), at the front on the 27th of September. Donovan took over from Tilney. As for Mitchell, from then on he conceived his role thus: he alone would take charge of replenishing supplies, Donovan could look after operations! Those few days at the outpost in a hut in the forest of Marimbois, close to the railway line built by the Germans, are still fresh in my memory. We ate outside on the kind of veranda the Germans favoured. My job, optional moreover, was to go up to the line every day to visit the 2nd Battalion deep in the forest of Dampvitoux. The 3rd Battalion were level with us to the north of the road from St. Benoît. Then, from 2nd Battalion Headquarters I went up to the line, where I would sometimes meet Donovan. I visited these small precarious emplacements, in the densely-coppiced forest. The line of resistance stretched out some 400 metres from the northern edge of the wood, where we had placed our advanced lookouts. Our nights were given over to very costly attempts at raiding the farm at Marimbois, the roof of which we could see on an outcrop 400 metres in front of the woods. These patrols regularly resulted in deaths, or worse, soldiers disappearing. We had most dramatic reports of the leader of the patrol visiting the farm and failing to bring back prisoners, an omission put down to over excitement. Yet the injured and dead bore witness to their efforts, however misguided they had been. Father Duffy's book is silent on the detail of all these massacres. Unsuccessful operations were systematically forgotten in that army. No blame was attached to anyone if the patrol or the reconnaissance unit returned with one or two soldiers missing.

Meanwhile, the Engineers worked on the line of resistance and on the second line; the former level with Louiseville Farm, the latter level with, and in front of, St. Benoît. We had taken the Dampvitoux Road and were posted on both sides of it. I still remember a visit to the Bois de Grande Souche, our outpost outside Haumont. I had to take a long detour in order to find the edge of the wood on the left hand side of the Dampvitoux road. Here I found Lieutenant Marsh with his company on a track reeking of mustard gas, the men bunched closely together as the Americans tended to, and what a sorry sight they looked. However, the lieutenant was kind enough to drive me to the edge of the wood where a burst of shell-fire gave us an unpleasant surprise. He had brought up his field kitchen to his company, but already the men seemed worn out by fatigue and fever. Without doubt, our setbacks in Argonne would prove to be the consequence of extreme fatigue, and this I now intend to describe.

Left to right: Captain Merle-Smith, Lieutenant Colonel Mitchell, Lieutenant Rérat, Lieutenant Leslie. The place and date are not identified.

The author, Armand Rérat, top right, pictured in 1918 when he was a lieutenant, with US Army officers.

Lieutenant Leslie, the Veterinary Officer, with the
Regimental Medical Officer; date and location unknown.

"The second person on my right, Tipheme."

A French tank, named 'Muette et Argonne', one of a number of photographs sent by the author to his parents. He wrote: "Here are a few photographs taken near the battalion's HQ. I am sending you this before going to the officers' class; then visiting Captain Aubry. Finally I will have to change my very dirty boots, get ready, etc., so I am in a rush. Sorry about this, my dears."

Captain Margot, French 223e Infantry Regiment with an anti-aircraft machine gun.

The author wrote: "Our Command Post at [Hill] 327. Our evening meal. The cyclist, back left, is Rigollet, my orderly. Note the heap of soil in the front; shelter freshly built in the hillside for the French PC, with entry protected from German shells by its orientation. The Germans could not see nor bombard it."

Opposite page: Cooks and orderlies with the author's battalion. Back row, left to right, Bourgeois (waiter), Desplanche (orderly to Lieutenant Lapierre), Pellus (groom), Besson (cook). Front row: left, Vernois (the captain's orderly); right, Rigollet (the author's orderly).

The church tower in Courbesseux(?), hit by a French shell.

A street in Chateau-Thierry, photographed on 6 February 1918.

A photograph sent by Armand Rérat to his parents, with the caption,
'Your son riding Jeanette'.

Le Foret de Parroy. The author wrote: "On the right, our colonel; on the left the commander of the battalion. In the centre Capitain Brosse. You can barely imagine the amount of mud, although it had been cleaned up in view of the colonel's visit. We are on the right path! If you follow the road on the right for 5kms you will get to the HQ."

Opposite page, below: A field kitchen, 'At the foot of Hill 327'. Meals and soup are cooked for the company during the march.

223e Infantry Regiment, Captain Margot (front row, centre) and his company

Officers, 223e, on the day the colonel departed. In the centre the colonel between the two Commandants'

'A quiet moment', from the author's collection. Armand Rérat is sitting on the left. Neither the location nor the other people in the photograph are identified.

The author's 'Hypokhâgne', H IV, 1910-11, in Paris. These two-year literary preparatory classes are renown in France for the highest level of training for admission to teacher training colleges etc. Armand Rérat is standing, second row, far right.

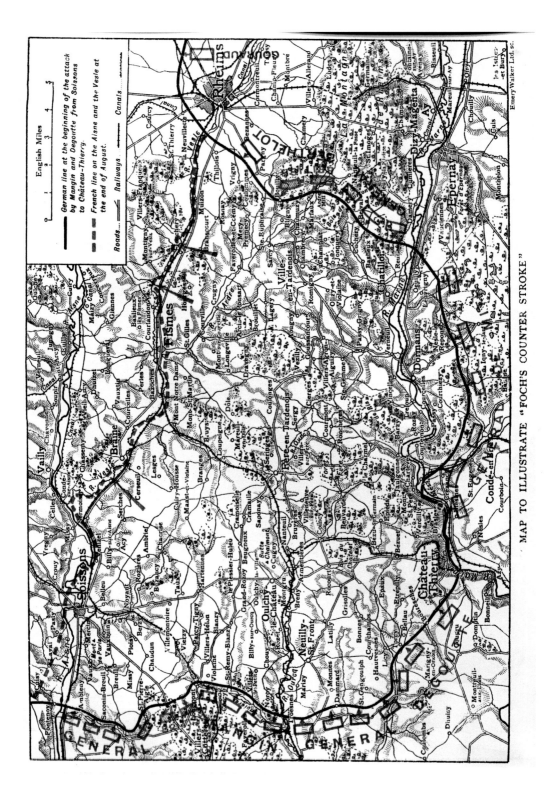

MAP TO ILLUSTRATE "FOCH'S COUNTER STROKE"

CHAPTER 4

The Argonne

THE REGIMENT LEFT the St Mihiel sector on the last day of September. We were transported in lorries to the region of the battle of the Meuse. Not a single one of our men had slept on straw since 8th September, in spite of our week's rest in the forest. Because of negligence and idleness at Headquarters we had camped in the mud, under dripping trees. Thus, even in quiet periods we had been no better off than at the front, not even secure since our woods were shelled every night. Indeed, a shell killed several men. I did try to obtain billets for our troops, but everywhere had been booked and occupied by the Artillery Corps. We could barely find accommodation for one battalion. In spite of our efforts the French were very mean towards us so that in the end our battalions camped in the open all round this small village. It was picturesque, but what a risk for these hundreds of tents in rows, with enemy planes flying overhead towards Bar-le-Duc and other towns behind the lines! This wretched hamlet on the Ayre river reminded me of Longchamp-sur-Ayre, of grim memory, where I had such a rough time with my French regiment in January 1917. Fortunately the weather favoured us, and had we stayed a few more days our men would have managed some sort of rest, even in such miserable quarters. Mondrecourt's inhabitants were poverty-stricken: half the village had been burnt in 1914. Being near the Voie Sacrée which could be seen from where we were, the poor village must have accommodated hundreds of thousands of men since 1914[13].

The distressing fact is that there was plenty of space to put the men in huts near other villages. But the American headquarters was not troubled by such petty details. The men were in tents: this made it so easy for everyone! As I said, the sun favoured us, and the nights were clear and beautiful. In the daytime I would go with Donovan to Souilly very nearby, where we bought food. Finally, on the 4th, orders to move arrived. Jubécourt was the first stage.

There again I tried to find good billeting for the troops, as I thought we might be allowed some rest. The Colonel and officers had excellent accommodation, and there were sheds in abundance to be rented out by the few inhabitants who had fled during the American offensive and were already back. Thus we were almost back to civilisation. Had the men been stationed in huts, the regiment would have been ready for new campaigns, after one week. Unfortunately, all the accommodation was monopolised by French artillery ammunition platoons. Camps everywhere; horses and men everywhere. Again, the whole 2nd Battalion had to camp out, disappointed because once more they did not get the huts they had been promised. They were fairly philosophical about it, however, and settled down along the stream. The rest of the regiment slept in the houses, under the eaves, thanks to me again: I had been so insistent that we got half the village to ourselves!

It was no use trying to settle down. We only spent one night in Jubécourt and continued our march towards the front. Closer together, always closer, seemed to be the single thought in this whole demented army. Troops pressed up against troops. The support division followed close on the one in front, as if to force it ahead. By doing this we cut between their food supplies and their ammunition. The infantry in the lines were hungry while the artillery had no shells. But divisions were at the ready, close to each other, well within range of enemy shells, and if by any chance a gap opened in the enemy line the Commander of the 6th Corps would push a little pawn with an imperceptible movement of his finger, and we would all be in the fray. How simple-minded they were at Headquarters! They wanted troops readily available, but ten kilometres from the lines was too far for these pathetic strategists. In Summerall's Corps, they were expecting to break through: I became convinced of this when we kept receiving those ignorant orders from that old-fashioned soldier.

What chaos on the scarcely repaired roads that crossed the former line level with Avocourt! Engineers were already mending the railway line. But just north of Avocourt, in the moonscape, a land turned upside down as if by an underground eruption, the roads were hardly eight metres wide. Further along, our march became easier, although with endless columns on every road it was in full view of enemy planes. The 42nd Division, after cutting through the food supplies of a fighting division for twenty hours, finally managed to cover the eight or ten kilometres from Jubécourt to the wood of Avocourt. I am not exaggerating: having left in the morning of the 5th, they arrived on the 6th, very late at night; not to mention that the food supplies took yet another day! But what a remarkable result had been achieved! Magnificent – the whole Division was well within reach of enemy 77s! It was level with the French 105 batteries, their sausage balloons, anti-aircraft batteries, artillery and Division Headquarters. At the front, the whole 42nd Division was at the mercy of heavy shelling and poison gas, having achieved nothing more than trapping the men in the lines and cutting them off from the rear, better and more efficiently than if we had been a German division.

As for us, instead of having a rest, we waited in this Montfaucon wood which had been ripped apart by the German artillery in February 1916, then again by our own artillery later. Not a single man could find a spot to set up his tent, because the shell holes ran into each other. For five days we remained stuck in the rain, the mud and the cold, staring at the aerobatics of the German planes which were attacking our balloons, listening to the roar of our guns and the enemy shells dropping at the edge of the wood. The Germans were kind enough to ignore us completely, even though this infantry brigade of 6000 men were massed on a few hectares of shell holes, with our Service Corps placed along the road and obstructing most of it: a fine spectacle to behold. However, it was a joy to see these thousands of fires, fed with the wood from a forest of jagged skeletons.

In the daytime, our men gathered round these hearths, which the Boche allowed us out of the goodness of their hearts, and they spent their time drying their clothes, wet from lying in the mud at night. Poor soldiers! I felt sorry for them. Crawling with vermin, they spent their time half-naked, delousing themselves. The regiment had dysentery and, as no latrines were set up, the wood became foul. Colonel Donovan held inspections to try and boost the troops' morale with vigorous speeches, but this was to no avail. They were overwhelmed by the vermin, the foul weather, the grim and unhealthy landscape and the badly-cooked food. Disease was rife and every day these poor young athletes decreased in number and fitness. Their muscles were failing; some, many, looked like skeletons. These poor naked, thin creatures were a pitiful spectacle, killing the vermin on their shirts like Sioux round their fires.

To crown it all, this was September but we had not yet received our greatcoats. We had one blanket per man, summer clothing and a raincoat in lieu of a greatcoat. Try and sleep out in the open in such ridiculous gear: the strongest constitutions could not have stood up to it. The guilt for this lay with everyone, but mostly with staff headquarters. Colonel Mitchell was no genius, to be sure, but he had long before reported the need for winter clothing. How guilty those headquarters were, wasting their excellent infantry, ignoring the basic rules of living in this way!

In fact we were all guilty, and we were led by ambitious men. If one had to assess the ravages and the massacres caused by monstrous ambition, I could put forward a powerful example: in France all our local offensives in 1915 were due to the frenzied ambition of senior officers. As for the Americans, their army headquarters were humiliated by this sudden blockage in their line at Montfaucon. It is always the case in an attack that after the first moment of surprise the enemy puts up some resistance. The American army was blocked outside Montfaucon. Moreover, there was nothing it could do: neither the artillery nor the infantry lines could receive ammunition because the roads were congested. To remedy this, fresh troops were thrown into the fray in the hope of using human flesh to compensate for the lack of foresight and the incompetence of headquarters. For them, it was easier to break through a fortified line at the cost of a number of human lives than to work out a sensible attack, showing caution and providence and giving coordinated orders. In this army they had soon got back to the easy solution of 'cannon fodder'. This enabled the headquarters staff to relax and live comfortably from one day to the next, while preaching sacrifice, courage, heroism, and praising those who were killed in action.

I seem to be exaggerating but this is indeed what happened. We were not thrown into the mêlée because there was no need: the German defence was faultless. The enemy felt harassed and were busy retreating; their rear was quiet, and not a single shell troubled our peace. I found a small PC for the Colonel, provided by artillery men. In our army it is natural for a Poilu to give his place to a colonel, but in the American army a colonel would never dream of asking this service from a soldier. With Mitchell I visited McCoy, whose brigade was not far away and grappling with the enemy outside Cierges. Though he was a Francophile, McCoy had no French second in command, although he had a French officer attached to each of his regiments. We were welcomed with open arms. How cordial he was! I am still moved when I think about this. On the way back, what a downpour! A deluge. Mitchell visited his former machine gunners, whom he found in a ravine not far from the Montfaucon Wood. All in all we had a good day.

What undermined our men's morale during these last October days was the big news that the Germans might be asking for an armistice. I did not believe this, or rather I thought it might be a ruse to end the war before they were defeated. I therefore ignored all the rumours, but the men lapped them up and believed in them with all their hearts. Donovan and Duffy showed a lot of common sense talking to the men and opposing the rumours. But the harm was done anyway: the fighting spirit in the regiment, the enthusiasm of the early days, both had vanished as they faced difficulties, dangers and endless suffering. Besides, the soul of the regiment had never sprung from anything other than overweening self-confidence. American morale had only been based on a wish to prove that they too were capable of fighting.

However, men worthy of the name seldom shrink from a challenge to show tenacity, to brave dangers without understanding why: these were the true reasons why soldiers kept going. Fleeing is wrong and not a single Frenchman or American wants to stay alive at the cost of admitting publicly that he is afraid and therefore a coward. In other words the notion of honour is so firmly fixed in every man that when the time comes he will do his duty after he has got over his initial recoil. I was not afraid my regiment might turn their backs on the enemy, but I knew that their drive, their spirit, the physical vigour which was so indispensable to their moral strength were very affected, very depleted. The first day of fighting would be hard.

Moreover the American officers who in normal times found it unnecessary to raise the men's morale were now so aware of the danger that they started preaching the idea of war, the impossibility of an armistice. They explained that soldiers should not be influenced by the idea of an armistice and should go on to the bitter end, failing which they would play into the enemy's hands. It is not a soldier's job to make decisions about peace.

On the 8th of October we went up and relieved, not the 32nd Division which was in front of us, but another American division that was more to the left, the 1st Division at Exermont, with the colonel's headquarters. The lines passed behind the village along the Côte de Maldat ridge, which stretched on the left of the village of Sommerance towards Flévelle. We did not know for sure whether either of these villages was occupied. The weather was abominable. On top of everything else, I caught the flu that was rampant at the time[14] and I received attention from the doctors of the French artillery, which was stationed next to the village. And so, during those first three days I was obliged to be a useless and unwilling witness of all the attacks and all the orders. I was forced to occupy for once the passive role that the Americans had always wanted of me. I did not go back to the lines until the 14th or the 15th; before then it was impossible in my state of health. I lay sprawled at the back of the cellar or would catch a breath of fresh air in the streets of this pitiful village. However, I found a shelter for Father Duffy on the first night. The Colonel nearly dismissed me as useless in the headquarters, along with others, including the sapper and an officer from the 37th. Although I was mad with rage at the time, I never realised how happy I might have been later about this. At least I would not have had to compromise myself by my presence, however honorary it was, and by my role as an extra, in this command post where orders arrived that would decimate the regiment. But unfortunately for me, the Colonel had a change of heart and kept me.

The attack was put off for two days. We had performed a relief action in readiness to attack but bad weather, rain, mud, cloudy skies, everything was against us. The French batteries had no ammunition and the American batteries no doubt even less. It may have been better for my peace of mind that I had no role to play. I felt there was something wrong, that we were not liaising with our neighbours on the front line either to the right or to the left. What could I do since I felt so weak? Even if I had been well enough to intervene and get my own information, would they have heeded my reports? Since the American success at St Mihiel, the French army had lost its brilliance in comparison with the Yanks. Moreover, at the staff headquarters they were doing their best to stir up American pride, which was becoming contempt for the French.

At St Mihiel, thousands of French officers, led by us people of the Mission, had come to visit the victorious site of this battle in which nobody actually fought. It appeared – something which we the witnesses did not know – the Americans had invented a new method for crossing the wired entrenchments. We had indeed heard before the attack about teams using light pontoons or similar methods, but apart from mortars producing a thick smoke screen a few minutes before the attack (an English method), I never saw anything original at St Mihiel. The whole thing was a parade manoeuvre.

In a word, we got what we deserved: we worshipped the Americans so much that they became stronger than their teachers and invented fighting methods of their own, to suit their temperament: in other words, no methods at all! As early as the 10th of October I was full of dark foreboding. I was more and more humiliated by the role they gave me. I would have loved to be among my people, in my regiment, and I was thinking sadly of how respected I was in my battalion, which I had forsaken for this wretched, uncivilised set of people. For it is sad to fight a war in this milieu. Their courage itself begins to irritate, for the bravery is playing to the gallery. I have never witnessed in the American army such spontaneous acts of dedication and complete self-sacrifice as we saw in our regiment.

It is true I have seen great soldiers, bold and heroic, but not with the wonderful bravery of the French who are well aware of the danger, clear-headed, their melancholy thoughts masked with a smile which hides the tears. There was the bravery of Baudet for example, a graduate of the Ecole des Mines (a prestigious educational institute in Paris), highly intelligent and cultured, who got himself killed trying to find out if the Boche had infiltrated into the ravine, although a number of victims had already been claimed by this reconnaissance attempt. Baudet, so far above the rest of us, was still not above performing the most humble task and did not think that dying like an ordinary soldier was too high a price to pay.

American courage was calculating, essentially theatrical and insincere. What gave them the implacable will to act was not lofty thoughts, but that fierce American pride to show that Americans can fight, as they said in their dispatches. Thus in the American army you never saw an artillery colonel going round the trenches at the height of battle to make sure that his fire was useful to the infantry. You never saw that generous behaviour, such as when Baudet accepted the most humble task to serve the country. To be sure, many would volunteer for patrols, but this was to show themselves off to their best advantage. In a word I have never come across this total, admirable self-sacrifice except among very young men and ordinary soldiers. Donovan, the bravest of them all[15], was consumed by ambition and worked on his fame in America: what was the point otherwise of so many newspaper articles published over there? He liked danger for its own sake, not to serve a cause; he liked it in the way of a supremely proud, admirable man who kept his self-control in the worst situations while others lost their heads. Donovan must have found subtle, intoxicating pleasure in braving danger and running risks, quite unlike the unthinking generosity of the French.

The principle among the Americans was to stick closely to the role they had been assigned. In this matter, American officers were mostly like the worst of the French leaders: a general never went to the lines except for effect, artillery men never tried to find out about the positions or needs of the infantry. As for the infantry, in the rear at the colonel's headquarters, they were not interested in what happened at the front in the lieutenant colonel's headquarters: every man for himself. Selfishness reigned supreme. Our artillery fired everywhere except on the enemy because they fired according to the map. The headquarters, having lost contact with the troops, were never informed whether the latter were tired or demoralised. To be sure, there was no lack of astounding bold individual performances. Leaders of men were many, particularly and surprisingly, among officers of German origin (Bootz for example in my regiment). But the exception confirms the rule: the American army was not a living body. It was heavy machinery in which each individual acted without putting his soul into it.

On the morning of the 12th we attacked Landres St Georges. As I suspected from the report of a patrol, which nobody else had noticed, the enemy had retreated as far as the Kriemhilde Stellung. About 2 kilometres of no man's land had been uselessly churned up by our artillery, while the position on the small rise in front of Châtillon (reinforced to the east by the peak of Châtillon), had been shelled only briefly. As I had also anticipated, our troops failed to follow our running barrage, and for lack of liaising with the 167th to our right at the start, we completely lost contact with the 84th Brigade. Donovan was happy to get all three battalions massacred with admirable spirit and courage. He relieved troops in full daylight, in the very middle of the battle, 200 metres from enemy machine guns. In short, though he could not be made responsible for the failure of the attack, as this was due mostly to inadequate artillery, it was his fault that so many men in the 165th lost their lives to no purpose. A proud soldier would have thought he had saved his honour after a first attempt and would have resigned himself to the impossibility of the attack. At the rear, headquarters were indifferent and did not intervene. Colonel Mitchell thoughtlessly dared to improvise a new, botched attack for the 18th, with Lenihan from the brigade. This is how our regiment were gallantly led to their deaths, and the assault to certain failure.

The Americans found it strange that Summerall from the Army Corps relieved both Colonel Mitchell and Lenihan of their duties. However, they both deserved it. They had recklessly agreed to ill-prepared new attacks called for by that frantic man Donovan. However, this was not the reason that Summerall relieved them, but because the assaults themselves failed. He came to visit us one night at Exermont. After the advances, I had warned Mitchell that he was mistaken in remaining so far from the front line – we were a good 4 kilometres away. Mitchell was happy being at Exermont, but it cost him his command and such a scathing reprimand that a French officer would have got himself killed the next day rather than survive the humiliation. Indeed, this was Summerall's advice to us. We French are reluctant to accuse the Americans of lacking balance and moderation to that extent.

Back at Headquarters, after the situation had been explained to him, Summerall was quick to call us all cowards. To serve his purpose he was even ready to take me to task, although I had no other function than that of liaison officer (my official title: I was liaising in this instance with the field artillery of this sector). My role had become less and less important, following the orders of this same general and Pershing's. Yet I too was hauled over the coals because Colonel Mitchell had positioned his headquarters further behind in a less dangerous zone, on a road accessible to his staff officers by car. If only Mitchell had listened to me that morning we would have been level with the village of Summerance, and out of range of the angry blasts fired by the general. Mitchell would have led his brave regiment back to America. Instead, he was relieved of his post.

In his harangue, which was indeed worthy of the American Civil War, I recall in particular that Summerall reproached us for not strewing the soil with our dead as the 1st Division had done, and for not forcing a way through, regardless of the cost. This fool would not accept what our four years of experience could have shown him, that not all assaults are possible. Outside Landres we were held up by a network of trenches ten metres wide. They were dense, intact and solid, and lined with a less difficult but still awkward system of traps. This was an insurmountable obstacle. The artillery's initial assault on the 13th October had been so feeble that, terrified by the hail of bullets, our troops had turned round and the tanks retreated 1500m before reaching the trenches. As for the first assault on the 12th, the Americans in their Renault tanks had arrived late. It was fortunate that these tanks belonged to the Americans: in the defensive action in Champagne on 15th July and in the offensive at Château-Thierry in August I had heard bitter criticism of the French. Our planes got the worst of it. The Americans cursed the French for their cowardice. For them, superiority in everything, including equipment of every kind, was paramount, and like spoilt children they would not tolerate anything that was second-rate. They even went as far as claiming that the only allied planes that had dared to fly over our lines in Champagne were not French, but English! This was very spiteful. This account of English planes at the front with the French 4th Army on the 15th of July is there for all to read in Father Duffy's book.

Summerall advised us to go and get ourselves killed the next day to redeem our honour, following the example of a colonel he named who, after a similar row with him, heroically led his regiment to death. I must admit I felt somewhat anxious for a moment. Luckily, Mitchell reacted well and displayed commendable good sense in this case. Twenty-four hours later he was relieved of his post.

Dravo, the lieutenant colonel in charge of the division's machine guns took over the command. His first move, on my advice, was to set up his headquarters farther forward, in what had been a German camp. I went to reconnoitre on the north slope of Hill 273. Mark Smith, the officer in charge of operations, had also been relieved of his post and Dravo decided to use me in his place. We spent these last end-of-October days on Hill 273. I have never seen anything as macabre as this German camp. Their huts, fetchingly done up in a variety of styles, were a real credit to our enemies. There were dear little forest houses with red roofs, clad in bark and moss, surrounded by miniature gardens and linked by a series of stairs and alleyways with handrails. The shelters were next to them or dug out of the side of the hut, which gave on to the hillside. Springs of fresh water at the foot of the camp supplied us as they had our enemies.

But what carnage! The huts were filthy with old dressings and in some, bodies were starting to decompose. It was an appalling sight. The dead seemed to be begging for life, frozen in attitudes of fear. But the Americans of the 1st Division had shown no mercy. After an advance in which they had left large numbers of their own dead on the southern slopes, mown down by German machine guns, they took this camp by surprise while it slept. The Germans came out panic-stricken, half-dressed, without their shoes and were massacred with pistols and bayonets. One can imagine the scene, the terror of unarmed men fleeing frantically in all directions, struck down as they ran. It was a sight I should never forget. Even at the first-aid post a man had been slaughtered on the steps, his head blasted open by a bullet while he was having a leg wound dressed. War is a filthy business, there is no doubt about it. Yet it is this kind of savagery which gives an army its reputation. The Americans showed no mercy and with bitterness they avenged the deaths of their comrades, now lying on the other side of the hill in front of the German machine guns.

Our 3rd Battalion, with Anderson acting as colonel, was opposite us on the other face, on Maldat Hill. The 2nd Battalion was in front of the hill, on the side which sloped down to a small ravine, facing the line of hills running east-west where the Boche were still holding out in front of Landres St Georges. Our men had dug themselves in as best they could in little copses, sheltered in steep-sided ravines lined with hedges, level with the village of Sommerance. They were on the receiving end of quite a number of shells, some of them mustard gas. The terrain was not really well thought-out. If discovered and attacked it would have been defended by only a few groups of machine guns in shell-holes. The men were putting on a brave face and considering the harsh conditions under which we had been living and still were, and the severe setbacks we had suffered, those who were left were holding out and keeping up their morale in the face of the most terrible hardships.

Things were easier where I was before, in my French regiment. On the most terrible days at Verdun, the messenger would come up to the front and, under a scrap of tent canvas between two tree-roots in Bois Fumin, we experienced the inexpressible joy of reading the lines from our dear ones. What a moment that was! A moment of Paradise in the midst of Hell. And after all, even there, weren't we always somehow or other sure of getting our supplies? Tins of cheap wine hastily thrown into shell-holes by men on fatigue duty, snacks of canned sardines and bars of chocolate, which it goes without saying nobody had much appetite for, bread rolls threaded on sticks or on lengths of string. But here, supplies had been non-existent for the first few days, until our field kitchens were set up behind Maldat Hill – at the bottom where they were hidden by bushes, the only traces of a forest razed by the Boche. Every day a meagre, miserable pittance came up and reached the combatants. In a sector like this our Frenchmen would have lived an almost normal life, but the Americans were completely cut off from the rear: not the slightest mail here, not even a newspaper at the colonel's headquarters. Yet, at this moment in the war the front was changing every day, the enemy retreating, and our morale would have been boosted by the good news that we so much needed.

You have to be an American to put up with so much deprivation. All in all these people have not created an army as good as ours, but the men had been trained in sports, resulting in an almost total lack of organisation. Having physical endurance enables people to hold out for some time, but here in this regiment it had come to a point where the spring of resistance is broken; our men were exhausted and demoralised. They only held on thanks to fierce energy, mostly among the leaders and a few others. Americans are a race whose individuals are of a strong constitution; their willpower makes up for errors inherent in hasty improvisation and compensates for the intellectual laziness of the leaders at all levels. It was a miracle that we were holding on: everyone was ill, suffering from influenza, dysentery, or the fever brought about by overwork. The French would not have survived under such conditions. In fact, what was happening here could be the mirror image of our first campaigns in 1914. I criticise the Americans, but I fully realise how admirable they have been to succeed to this extent, however relative their success. The men we had left were the best, the officers too, and the regiment gave me many reasons to admire them during the twenty days before the armistice.

Most of all I admire Bootz, this German, barely Americanised, with such a precise mind, though hardly any culture. He speaks English with a German accent and I imagine he writes to his father in the States in German, like other officers I know. This does not stop him saying that if he was confronted by one of his brothers he would kill him without remorse – for he has brothers in Germany. The worst of it is that he would assuredly do so. He was a non-commissioned officer in peacetime and has dedicated himself to the American army entirely. I went to visit him one fine morning and found him in his headquarters by the brook that flows towards the west from Châtillon Hill. His headquarters was concealed behind a few trees, in a big shell hole. To get to that advanced point I had to cross a ridge only 1500m from German machine-guns. The Germans, watchful as ever, recognised me as an officer in my sky-blue uniform, and sprayed me generously while I was taking shelter in a shell-hole. Fortunately I was able to find cover in a small copse. I steered clear of open country after this! Bootz explained his position with clarity: he at least knew and understood the art of command. At the top of Maldat Hill we had a fine observation point over enemy lines, but it was not a healthy spot to linger. Back at headquarters Dravo wanted to live in a 'cagna'[16] to show off. He was a braggart. Nevertheless, a few days later at the Arietal Headquarters, after his hut had been destroyed and fell on his head, he was the one to show the most extreme example of caution, spending his nights in a small trench.

Around the 25th we moved to the right and relieved the 84th Brigade; the 166th Regiment took our place. The 84th at least did good work. While we managed to get decimated outside the barbed wire, they took the important Châtillon Hill, right inside the Kriemhilde Stellung, thus making a deep breach in the German line of defence. This is where we relieved them. Every day there was talk of an attack by the 42nd, 'Rainbow' Division, *with Douglas MacArthur, who had been promoted to brigadier general in July.* In the meantime we reinforced our artillery and ammunition arrived. We brought our batteries nearer, into the Bois de Romagne, a wood razed to the ground as they all were, and in full view of the enemy. Could the Germans have foreseen when they wrecked and wiped out our forests, that this would be another asset if they retreated, as they would be able to follow our movements better in the Ardennes Forest? Or did they only act out of greed, to make France poorer while they were getting richer? The fact is, our unfortunate batteries were soon spotted when they ventured on that terrain, and they suffered many losses.

Yet it seems Summerall finally decided to do things right and resume modern warfare, instead of primitive hand-to-hand fighting, as he had recommended. At any rate his anger was justified: Foch had visited Pershing, then both went to Summerall. Foch, the Allies 'generalissimo', was not an easy man. In his opinion things were not going well and the American army was not making any progress: indeed, since the September 25th offensive we had gained very little ground. We got word of the generalissimo's anger: we had to be at Buzancy by November 1st. But Buzancy is some 14km north! Each battalion in the regiment was reduced to 300 men on average, all exhausted or ill. Yet they claimed that this much depleted force would succeed, so long as they were supported by good artillery preparation.

We were in our new headquarters, in another German camp, without shelter, not on a hillside, but in a wood level with the Ferme d'Arietal, 3 or 4km south of Châtillon Hill. There we relieved the 167th. Our headquarters consisted of a tall, solid building made out of split logs which also formed the ceiling, In fact these buildings would withstand shelling by the 77s, as experience would prove. Every night in our forest we got pummelled by sporadic bursts of shells, mostly gas, but you are not fully aware of this in such a sheltered wood. We slept any old how, all headquarters officers and liaison officers together. When the Boche suddenly woke us, for a few moments we would get the unpleasant feeling that goes with being shelled, but fortunately the blankets and the warmth and comfort in the building seemed to protect us, even against the shelling. Only on one night did everyone get up, terror-stricken, when a shell hit the Colonel's hut, which was just like ours. Its men went and slept in the ditch at the edge of the forest. This is something I would never have done: I had learned to prefer proper rest to relative safety without comfort.

Our battalions were further from us. 500 metres north, Anderson occupied headquarters buried in a very steep ravine, not far from the road that winds along the main valley. Our 1st Battalion was with the support battalion, against the south wall of the Petit Bois crest, very steep and sheltered from the attacks. The men could easily be seen from the planes, for here again the wood had been razed to the ground. All their tents could be seen from miles away. Surprisingly, German planes left those masses of men on the slope completely alone. The Boche hardly reacted; the troops in the rear had quietened down, and in the daytime we were very seldom disturbed. Yesterday however, I visited Mercier at the brigade and he walked a bit of the way back with me. Suddenly, near the Ferme d'Arietal a volley of large shells gave us such a shock that we took to our heels.

The time for aerial battles had come. German planes, although greatly reduced in numbers, were as bold as ever. Their losses must have been heavy. Our anti-aircraft batteries were very active, and I had already seen two or three planes shot down in a few days. I witnessed one terrible scene that I will remember for ever: a flight of daring German predators came and attacked a peaceful reconnaissance of humming American aircraft, manoeuvring in triangular formations. I heard the faint sound of German machine guns and I looked up to see the swarm of planes swirling, then put to flight and the bluish streaks of the tracer bullets in the sky as the enemy fled, satisfied with the attack. Then suddenly I had the impression there had been a disaster. High in the sky I saw something that looked like leaves falling in autumn. My vision became blurred and I thought the whole squadron was swirling and crashing down. Among this debris, some floating like wings, was one shape I recognised – the fuselage of a plane was tumbling down at a wild speed towards the ground, engine first. But a heart-breaking vision was that of a human being falling behind, pirouetting from high in the sky like a minute clown, its feet first then its head, and its legs torn apart by the speed. It was a man, still alive perhaps. For a moment I forgot that this man would be unconscious and would not feel anything. My heart stopped, I was terror-stricken until this fearsome sight disappeared.

Dravo was not showing off to us anymore. This 'bravest of the brave' was forever dreaming up coups, and every night some patrol lost one or two men. I was supposed to be in charge of operations with him, but he only consulted me to ask for my agreement to some criminal, ambitious extravagance: surprise attacks with a short artillery preparation every night, and every night with a negative result and adding up to losses. I tried to moderate his criminal orders. But on no account could I talk him out of these costly, unsuccessful endeavours, for I would then lose my influence. Bootz then Reilly were relieved on line. Reilly got the 'flu and was evacuated; his battalion was then commanded by Merle-Smith who had come back. Fortunately I had a friend at the headquarters, Meaney, second in command to the Colonel. He was sensible and this was a comfort. Finally I had my Greek orderly, who used to be in the Foreign Legion; he was dedicated and I asked the Colonel if I could have him. As a soldier with four years' experience of warfare, a 'Médaille Militaire' and several decorations, it seemed to me that he should have been at least a non-commissioned officer. Buck, his company commander, was not even employing him as a liaison agent – he was my man.

My job consisted in moderating Dravo's temper. When he was willing to give me the chance, he let me go to find out what was happening at the front. Apart from Irving, I was the only one at the Colonel's headquarters who visited our trenches. As far as I knew the Colonel did it only once. This sword-swallower astonished me when one day he asked me to accompany him to the trenches and put the question, "Do you know the way?" He had never been before and this was the only time. Finally we had Irving, reserved, reliable, modest, hard-working. He was in charge of 'Inquiries'. As for me, I would go to the lines on my own when I felt like it, but it was far from pleasant. One day I was caught in the Bois de Romagne by a barrage so sudden and intense that I thought my last hour had come. However, I had the pleasure of meeting Irving, nestling with his observers in a shell-hole! Nothing is as cheering as such encounters at the very moment when you believe you are going to perish, alone, in a corner like a dog.

At the front our men were placed at the edge of the Bois de Châtillon and scattered inside the wood. A few were perched on the very top of the isolated hill, and from this summit we could see Landres St Georges and the whole German line as if we had been there. In the distance, on the Chenery road, a few Germans were having a nonchalant stroll, others making their way cautiously in small groups or on their own. This peak was an ideal observation post for the artillery but nobody was using it. Nothing much was left of the village itself and the houses were jagged ruins.

Those were melancholy days. The war had never been more hateful, more implacable. And we had never seemed further from the end. This shows that men who are in the thick of events are not capable of judging them soundly. At Chaumont, three days before the armistice, our troops took about twenty prisoners on the heights above Sedan; they were the remnants of a German company. I can still see their procession as they carried the wounded on stretchers, among them an officer who did not survive. I questioned the non-commissioned officers: their orders had been to withdraw that same evening (November 10th) to the other side of the Meuse. But their persistence in defence was to their credit, even though the line had collapsed. Thus they had sacrificed themselves for the cause of their country, a handful of men facing our battalions. I marvelled at their gallant resistance. Although their retreat gave me courage and the hope of a prompt ending to the war, I could not refrain from comparing this evidence with reports from villagers who would show us heaps of broken rifles, telling us that the end had already been proclaimed in Germany and that things had got out of hand.

In fact, troops on the front held on to the last day, such is man's sense of honour. Retreating from the enemy and behaving like a coward to save one's life, in front of others, is something no man worthy of the name can bring himself to do. This is why courage is not rare, but true heroism is. Mankind is better than one is usually inclined to think. Narrow-minded people have slandered it. But great men were never fooled and trusted human nature completely, because its essence is generosity and forgetfulness of self. Men forget themselves as individuals. The fear of discipline or court martial would not make them resist the enemy, nor the habit of four years of combat. To explain these countless deaths, this supreme sacrifice by a whole generation, let us perhaps look to this sublime sense of honour which makes people confront the worst tortures and death itself rather than shame.

CHAPTER 5

The Final Days of the War
German Oppression

O N THE DAY of the armistice I was not deliriously happy, unlike some others. There, with the Americans, I was pleased, very pleased it was all over. In fact, joy is always contagious, not something you can keep to yourself. It should only be displayed openly. But that was not the case at Brigade headquarters with the Americans: the 12th of November was a day like any other. For two days we had been travelling away from Sedan, once more crossing through the wretched countryside we had just liberated. On the day of the armistice we arrived just at the edge of the zone that the Germans had cleared, and so we were occupying an uninhabited village that had been looted. I must recount briefly my final impressions of the War.

During these final days, my regiment had filled me with pride. The few men who had survived had formed themselves into very manageable, also very reliable, units. I was there at their advance from Chaumont to the Bois de la Loupe on the 9th of November, and I could only admire them for their skill in using the terrain, for their inspirational courage, their cohesion and harmony. The 37th came to the aid of the infantry, the machine gunners protecting them by well-aimed fire at the Germans who were visible on a bare hillside, which on the other side dropped down to the Meuse. We had ended the war with brilliant performances by the infantry, this time not paid for in lives, but earned by skill rather than by great numbers, and by superior manoeuvres rather than by force. We had managed not to pay dearly for such 'fine exploits' as driving out the enemy in full daylight from heights, which in any case he would be evacuating that night.

There was no lack of initiative on this occasion. Anderson carried out some clever infiltration manoeuvres, which almost succeeded. Only Merle-Smith, blundering as usual, had spoiled our plans. He had made contact with a French artilleryman and, without informing anyone, ordered him to open fire on the southern edge of the Bois de la Marfée. As a result we were never able to take this position, even when the German machine-gunners were dislodged. In addition, because of this action by the 75s (*the French artillery*), our losses on the plateau to the east of the wood were quite considerable. I had to look for the artillery command post, and by nightfall I eventually found the major who was busy firing at the same blessed wood. He had held us up and also greatly demoralised us – all because of Merle-Smith's wrong information. That same evening one of our patrols, in spite of losses caused by the line of German machine-guns on the other side of the River Meuse, pushed on as far as Wadelaincourt. They returned only when they had accomplished their mission, but only one man had been able to get through to the end. The arrival of our relief on the night of the 9th and 10th of November would have afforded us a well-earned rest, if the armistice had not intervened.

At Brigade Headquarters, Mercier was furious at being replaced on the day of the armistice. Truth to tell, he had complained of not being able to get along with the General. He remained at headquarters for a few days until he knew the whereabouts of his next American brigade, and then we set off together. I was extremely tired and found the slog through the pot-holes and craters in the road arduous. Patou[17] caught up with me when I was billeted with the brigade at Chémery. On the 11th of November we were quartered at Petites Armoises on the main highway; on the 12th we completed a long stretch as far as Thénoignes, and I recall all the details of our journey. We came upon a German burial ground at Brieulles which only a few days earlier had been the combat zone. Recent burial plots, the newly dug earth already sinking into the graves, lay to the side of older graves, which the Germans, with great respect for their dead, had found time to decorate.

At Verrières I had to intervene in order to prevent an unbelievable waste of thousands of sacks of flour from a German-held mill. A stream of people from the region were gathering there to stock up: women, children, old folk with wheel-barrows and sacks of all sizes. My protest was not about this, but about what was happening inside the mill. Being unable to carry the heavy 100 kilogram sacks, each person would empty onto the ground half or two thirds of the flour, then take away what remained. Everyone was tramping around up to their knees in an ocean of dusty grey German flour. Forcefully, I demanded that the mayor put an end to this appalling waste, and made it quite clear to him that there was not a surfeit of flour in France, any more than there was in Germany.

Further on, when I arrived in Fontenoy, it was the Americans who suffered the effects of my anger. This was the first uninhabited town, and we were billeted there. American engineers were everywhere, repairing the roads, but you would never believe the way these uncivilised troops were going about it. They had started out making use of stone from garden walls: I said nothing. If you discounted the pillaging of furniture by the Germans and some shell holes, this village had been almost untouched. I then discovered a team of engineers busy demolishing a very beautiful house which up to this point had remained unscathed. In order to do this, they were making use of a breach in the wall made by a German shell. Here again it was my duty to protect our national heritage. I had to intervene again the next day at Thénorgues, where they were keeping warm by burning furniture. However, the damage that I saw and that which I prevented was an infinitesimal fragment of the ruin which was destroying the Ardennes region. Everywhere the trees had been stripped bare by ill-fed, starving American mules. Timber, floor boards and furniture were being burned indiscriminately, and with a savage indifference, because of the shortage of wood. What the Germans had started the Americans were continuing.

It was on the 12th November that we learned from the sappers that the armistice had been signed, although for a while we thought it was one of those false rumours that had been circulating for several days. I believe it would have meant nothing to me without Mercier's company, but being together increased our joy, and in the end we spent an agreeable day making plans for the future. The next day I got hold of a car from the command post. After first stopping at Récicourt, we managed to get as far as Bar-le-Duc, although the car was in such a bad state I never thought we would make it. That is how the war ended for me. I remember the wide, white road, the 'Sacred Way', that had saved Verdun in 1916. We had to push the car up all the hills! Eventually we left behind us the silhouettes of those cold, desolate, yet proud hills which lie along the Sacred Way, and arrived at last in the Barois, a less deserted, less militarised region.

After a night spent in the officers' mess in the town and travelling onwards by railway, I had the totally unexpected good fortune to meet Rendu, my Commandant of the 230th on the train. I fell into his arms. From the restaurant car window I saw at first hand the ravaged countryside of the Marne as it passed by. This jewel of France, this rich, luminous valley – how this region had suffered! The ruins I saw were wealthy villas in more prosperous successful times before the war. It was this area that revived our men's morale when they were able to escape the Battle of Verdun in 1916 for a period of rest. It gave them renewed courage to face death. 'Yes! France is a country worth dying for!', was the cry heard from soldiers on leave as the train rattled through the fertile, peaceful banks of the Marne. The Germans had reached the most beautiful area of France in 1918, and they had laid it to waste. This was the price we had to pay for defeating them and the ruins were still there to be seen.

Whilst on the train, Rendu spoke to me about the courage shown by the Regiment, where every man played his part in the action. I was filled with admiration for our comrades as he mentioned name after name. Kind-hearted Lapierre, who led the battalion on two occasions, became a hero – he was the only officer to survive. Fontanel, Gallic hero, overtaken by bad luck in 1918, gassed, unable to leave the battle for several days although blinded – another Oedipus, with a soldier leading him by the hand. Fontanel was a victim of German mustard gas, not of the anger of the Gods, nor Destiny, but of Man's struggle for Liberty. More names came and went during Rendu's account, names which brought a lump to my throat as I heard them. They included Baudet, hero of engagements and hero of the retreat from the Aisne, who fell so gallantly, volunteering to reconnoitre a position infiltrated by the Germans. Poor Baudet, noble friend whose esteem was an honour! With his mocking humour he hounded all rogues, cheats, cowards, the petty, the feeble-minded, but had boundless friendship for those who showed dedication and a sense of duty. He loved the high life but had the soul of a Spartan; he was a materialist but knew that only things of the spirit really mattered.

Listening to my commander and also telling him my impressions of the American army, I could not help regretting what I had lost, a year among good people, all decent Frenchmen. Nothing can equal the bravery, the dignified dedication of a French regiment. Would it not have been better to have died with them, died like them, as Fate decreed, rather than accepting this task, useful certainly, but thankless, and among foreigners too? For the Americans were becoming more and more foreign to me. The gulf between us deepened despite the generosity with which they surrounded me, and despite the popularity I enjoyed, at least among the officers. I had lost contact with that refined French culture, hidden away in the soul of even the most ordinary of my countrymen – an eloquent humour, an engaging, lively, alert mind, always witty and not without great and beautiful ideas. I recall that in accepting the role of instructor with an American regiment, I certainly held a privileged position, exerted a wide-ranging influence and I served my country usefully. However, speaking personally, I lost what a Frenchman finds most precious, those honest, loyal friendships that come from fighting in a French regiment.

I would never see my regiment again, and this bereavement was the price I had to pay to get to know the Americans.

CHAPTER 6

The Rhine

AFTER THE ARMISTICE I was no longer attached to the 165th, but transferred to the 83rd Brigade. However, I did not lose all contact with my comrades during the last months of the war, as they remained in the vicinity of the brigade and I often visited them. When I returned from leave early in December I found my new Brigade with the 165th Infantry at Useldange, an attractive village near to the city of Luxembourg. Because we were their liberators, the people of Luxembourg gave us a warm welcome. They were very generous in their show of friendship; the Germans in the community were doubtless keeping a low profile. To us, Luxembourg felt like France. I clearly remember feeling that we had set them free – at least that was the impression they gave us. I could imagine the relief, after four years of subjugation under the German yoke, no longer to feel that burden, to be delivered from that servitude.

From my first day here, I could see that the countryside did not seem to have suffered from the effects of war. I travelled by car from Chaumont to Metz, following the River Moselle. Passing through Lorraine – now French Lorraine – I carried out some small investigations, questioning people and seeing for myself the effects of fifty years of 'Germanisation'. The Lorraine people were no longer able to understand French, even though the old folk had known it in the past. However, some managed a few words in order to show us the way. I should think that the language would come back to them quickly because before the War, French was widely spoken throughout this region. On the other hand, in Luxembourg, where French had not been forbidden during the war, people spoke French. These Luxembourgers were delightful and they naturally took on French nationality. Flags were every-where, just as in the villages of Lorraine. Whereas the Americans had the impression that these people were courteous, but rather cold, I felt they were all our friends. They gave the impression that you just had to ask them and they would take French nationality. Everywhere we had a touching welcome from these excellent folk! Wherever I was billeted on my way towards the German border they were pleasant, courteous and kind, although here more and more people spoke German,. One day as I was leaving, the locals from one of the spotless houses offered me some apples, bread and butter. They knew not one word of French and spoke to me in their local dialect which I barely understood. Luxembourg had not suffered much damage despite air-raids aimed at the viaduct. However, although the town remained intact, the air-raids had caused many civilian casualties. They did not complain: the bombardments were a military necessity.

It was most amusing to note the curiosity I aroused as I made my way across the fields. If I passed close by a farm, everyone from the farm would come out to meet me uttering great cries of joy. I had to stop and talk to the farmer and his workers in pidgin French. These gestures of friendship were made to us French: the Luxembourgers were more cold towards the Americans, and the same old quarrels between their troops and the civilian population manifested themselves once more. Of course, parity of the German Mark was obligatory and prices everywhere were exorbitant, especially for such scarce commodities as leather and soap. The Americans did not like paying these high prices! I could tell the same old tale of minor thefts by the Americans and of complaints from the locals about damage of all kinds done during our short stay in Luxembourg. However, our passage through the region was not always disadvantageous to the locals. They somehow managed to trade food for pairs of shoes. This small-scale, yet brazen trading disgusted me so much that I almost intervened; but after all, it was nothing to do with me. If the American officers were turning a blind eye, too bad for them.

Having been prepared for it by gradual changes on the way, our arrival in Germany was not a surprise. My first contact with Germany left me with the memory of a prosperous little town, crowded streets swarming with children, where people watched us passing through without any alarm. From my first billet in Germany I remember the young girl and her brother, a sailor. They were both extremely decent obliging folk and both deplored the war. One of the things the girl asked me was if she would soon be able to go to see the grave of her other brother, a German officer who had been killed in Champagne. These people were quick to say that the Americans were not true soldiers – that is, not Prussian-style soldiers. For example, they were surprised that cooks did not salute correctly when officers entered the kitchen. Quite the contrary, they jostled them. They said that their cooks would stand to attention. It cannot be denied that our advance into Germany did not impress the local people. Our mangy, under-nourished horses were exhausted. Carcasses lay scattered along the roadside, still unburied, several days after the American 1st Division had passed through ahead of us.

I state here and now that the Americans got on well with the Germans: they were made to get on together. To begin with, their racial history made them closer to the Germans than ever the French could be. From the moment we arrived in Germany I could hear unpleasant comments about France being shouted out loud for my benefit. The villages here were cleaner, with no huge dung heaps. On the other hand this was not true of the poor, mountainous villages we were passing through. These villages looked wretched and the houses quite squalid, but even so the Americans were inclined to admire everything. It is true, the railways were better, the stations huge, the level-crossings more modern. One soldier remarked in particular that here it only took one lever to open both gates, whereas in France you have to wait five minutes for the old crossing-keeper to open both sides!

In the inns, German-born American officers and men got on well with the locals, and you could feel a sense of harmony. I would not have advised adopting a hostile attitude, but in my opinion, things went too far. Eventually, back at Brigade Headquarters, I complained about the lamentable state of things. The new general had just arrived from America, and consequently he had seen nothing of the war. Neither had his administrative staff, being composed of two young lieutenants. Luckily three officers I knew from Colonel Reilly's staff were still there: Martin, in charge of liaison, Lindsay the Scottish vet, and the Chief of Staff. At least these men were not hostile towards me. However, the general and his two acolytes had a grudge against me, and as far as they were concerned I was an outsider. They made sure I knew it too, by allocating me the worst billet imaginable. In the end, angry and hurt not so much for myself personally, but in order to redeem French pride in the eyes of the Germans, I went to find the general. He did recognise, albeit begrudgingly, that I had the right to the best room after the captain, the commander and himself. It took several weeks for this coolness between us to dissipate, and in the meantime I had no end of a job to ensure that my orderly travelled by lorry. Everything they could refuse me they did.

The general brought into the Brigade a poorly educated machine-gun officer. He was the worst example of a German-born American, combining the worst faults from both countries: German servility with American coarseness. For example, I had to speak to him sharply to get any respect from him. General Coldwell left by car accompanied by this 'Boche' disguised as an American. It was no privilege to be with Coldwell, who was a narrow-minded minor tyrant. Amusingly, MacArthur had this to say about him and he was probably quite correct: "The best thing Coldwell made was his two daughters". At any rate, at meal times, as soon as he arrived, the General greeted everyone with an icy stare, he would never smile, and no one dared joke or laugh in front of him. He was the most hateful type of military man I ever met. He thought only in terms of discipline and men were valued for their rank alone. It was under the despotism of this person that I was to end my military career.

CHAPTER 7

German Oppression: Under the Yoke
The Relief of Ardennes

IT IS FOUR months since the war finished and soon the memories of those long days of suffering will fade, become blurred and vague. It must surely be important, before it is too late, to fix in the memory the richest, finest emotions human life has to offer. Yes, there really were fine days in this war. And the most terrible times do not leave the most painful memories. I will start with an account of my last campaign days. This final period, the defeat of the Boche and the return to a war on the move, ended so abruptly with the armistice that the French in the rear were taken by surprise. The newspapers had little to say. One example from my own experience will give a brief idea of what literature and the history books will have to tell later.

My American division, after four days of rest, had relieved another division which was on the enemy's tail. The situation was clear after our violent 1st November attack. The French were attacking in the west in Argonne, the Americans were east of the famous forest below Buzancy. The enemy were withdrawing rapidly towards the Meuse and only the river could protect them for a short time. Their exhausted troops could no longer hold out against the formidable waves of attack, the aerial bombardments, the hail of bullets and the steady, courageous advance of the Poilus and the Yanks. And yet this terrain could not have been easier for the Germans to defend: there were deep valleys and hills, steep but not like mountain peaks, which would have allowed them to resist if there had been enough men. The front was collapsing everywhere. Even Lorraine, around Nancy, would become a battleground. The Boche were moving out. We joined the relieving force just outside the first village still to be evacuated. From 5th to 10th November, every day we passed Boche rearguards who held out just long enough to allow their artillery to retreat to other positions.

The advance proceeded without any fighting, but our suffering was considerable. The bridges had been blown up and the smallest stream became an obstacle. Our field kitchens struggled to reach us until well into the night. As for artillery, after advancing for twenty-four hours, we had none. The railway embankments had been blown up, overhead bridge-ways collapsed onto the roads' All these many obstacles, including the cleared forest paths and trails (log roads made as only the Boche knew how), were all destroyed by mines. It was enough to make our starving infantry feel wretched, but how would our young Americans face it? Some ate cabbages and beet from the fields. At night they slept in some furrow or other or under a hedge. No fire, no food, no roof over their heads. The land stretched out, like a desert. The Germans, foreseeing defeat, had not done any autumn planting. So, what about the civilians, you are saying. Well, the land had ceased to belong to the civilians a long time ago. They had long since renounced their worldly goods. The Masters had taken it all and this Ardennes countryside which had been theirs for four years was now a desert, bare and wasted. Not a soul to be seen… …but yes! Here is a civilian!

Slate roofs appear on the ridge across from us. Our troops are advancing in small formations. A German machine gun fires from long range, but the bullets fall wide. A man runs towards us, coming from the village where white flags are flapping; he is delirious with joy and rushes into the arms of the first soldier. He has come to tell us that the Boche is gone and we can advance without fear. *Yes, go to the village, quick; they are all waiting for you; you will be welcome!* Stoically our troops keep marching past this offer of shelter; they cannot stop. But I, being with the Colonel, do not have to follow the leading patrol, Surely I can find a moment to go and visit our fellow Frenchmen, rediscovered at last. When I started to march this morning, it promised to be hard, without food or rest, and I did not expect to feel such emotion – in this village, through which our troops are still marching, I am the only French soldier.

Women are bustling about, serving coffee to anyone in sight, making food for the hungry and those who have time to stop in all this excitement. But when they see my sky blue uniform they stop in their tracks: *Look, there is our saviour!* I then become the centre of a growing crowd! Women, young girls, men, all clasp my hands, hug me, and talk from their hearts, which open for the first time in four years. I am the joy they had lost, I bring them the speech which was useless with the Americans. I am inundated with questions, tugged this way and that. They all want to corner me, take me to their homes, give me a bed and a meal. I have to eat, at least to drink, drink coffee. Coffee in every house in the village, in all these homes where people, evacuated from the North, Lille, Armentières, Roubaix, Lens, have come to join the families of Ardennes villagers. I drank so much coffee that I was unable to sleep for several nights. What joy, what overwhelming happiness!

Straight away of course, after their first words about joy and gratefulness and love of France, they started talking of their sufferings. I heard so many stories! In all these villages I went through everyone had their own personal account to tell, their own cause for resentment against the enemy. Their hatred was justified, their misery took a hundred different forms, their tales of suffering were inexhaustible. But in all these stories there was a common feature that was a feeling of hatred towards the enemy. That hatred was justified, well thought-out; their resentment was fostered by factual arguments provided by the Germans themselves. Furthermore there was a sort of defiance of the enemy. Deep down they had kept their mocking, satirical attitude, their anger toward the Boche, their indignant badinage, the which often became defiance. The thousand and one ways our French people have to express their independence in the face of constraint, their disgust in spite of threats, all this muted rebellion against the invader could be material for a really fine book.

Boche oppression was not always successful and never triumphed over people. In truth, I only saw one area where civilians were really broken, body and soul, by the iron hand. It was in St Mihiel in the small villages behind the front: Essey, Pannes, poor wrecks of villages. I shall always remember that pitiful woman, terrified at the thought of cooking food for the Colonel on the day of our victorious advance. *No, I can't!* She was a patriot. *But a colonel! Haven't you got a cook, then? My food wouldn't be good enough! It's impossible!* And although I stressed that he was not a German colonel and if she did not cook us a meal we would have to leave with empty stomachs, stubbornly she kept refusing, her eyes wide with fear at the thought of displeasing the Colonel with poor quality food, *'popote' (poor quality food)*. There was also that poor little French boy who announced proudly that his father was employed by the *Kommandantur*. Doing what? *Oh!* the little boy said, *he would clean the streets, sweep the leaves…*Poor child! The Boche had taught him to be proud to be a slave. Or – but this would be another story – at St Mihiel, people spoke the German war language and used all the military Boche words. Aircraft were *Fliege*, the cinema was a *Kino, and* so on. It was sad speaking to those poor,

111

broken creatures in whom the Boche had planted and nurtured terror and an unimaginable degree of respect for their officers. They were those German Gods' unhappy slaves. They were stagnating at a level even inferior to that of German soldiers. The Boche had kept them there, in their villages, as protection from our shells, knowing full well that we would be unwilling to shoot as long as we knew there were civilians in a village. During their offensive in the spring of 1918 they were in a rush to evacuate towns and villages from the salients they had created, in order to plunder and ransack them, but they were determined not to evacuate our villages at the front that had been ruined or annihilated by four years of trench war. This is another story, yet again.

Deep into the interior the Germans had subjugated civilian populations everywhere. Our country had become their possession. As they often boasted – and this came back like a chorus in their arguments – weren't they the victors? Weren't they the masters? How fast we French are to forget: we had hardly been in Germany for three months (*Remagen*) and we had already forgotten that we were the Masters, if we ever thought we were[18]. Yes, dominating, oppressing, enslaving are not in our temperament but a little tyrant lies dormant in the soul of every German. I must say this however, these people in the Argonne were unanimous in never complaining about soldiers. One example a mayor gave me will be enough to prove that the Germans' great respect for discipline made it logical and necessary for them to punish the slightest damage to property. The mayor of Authes told me that the Boche seldom or never plundered as individuals, as this was forbidden. In 1914 a soldier had stolen vegetables from a garden. His captain had him tied to a tree, gathered his company in front of the victim and announced that the next thief among his men would not suffer such a light punishment. *No*, he said, *I would blow his brains out*. One thing was sure: our peasants were sensible enough not to underestimate the military worth of our enemies. They admired it even during the war, even under the German heel.

An honest Frenchman could differentiate between the German army and the German government. He believed the army to be strong and well disciplined (the mayor could give me many examples of this), Yet he could not find words strong enough to condemn the meanness, cupidity and greed of the German people, as personified by the *Kommandantur*. I wonder if we realise in this country and if we keep the image ever-present in our minds, that our invaded regions were thoroughly sucked dry, as the Shakespearian stone marten sucks an egg until only the shell is left? Newspapers have often said this, but we can barely believe it. I knew the Germans made requisitions from time to time, but I still imagined I would find rich peasants, prosperous in their trade with the Germans, cultivated land and fine cowsheds. But who could have dreamed of such devastation? If the war had spared them, these poor people had only their roofs and furniture. Every last one of their animals and their tools had long since been taken. The Germans organised slavery as it had not been seen since earliest antiquity. These people had no possessions. Freedom was non-existent: they could not even go to the next village. Passes were only given for work which was for the benefit of Germany. In any case this was the only work there was. I have heard so many complaints about this one subject! For instance one woman had not seen her mother for two years, and her husband lived in the neighbouring village. From a fixed time, usually eight p.m., nobody was allowed to be in the street. Several times during the day they had to answer a roll-call at the whim of those in the Kommandantur. If you missed roll call you got a fine of several Marks. The mayor of Authes told me that in his little village, of 800 inhabitants, they had paid over 30,000F in fines.

The Germans lived with local people who were forced to show them consideration, perfect politeness, whether it was at home or in the street. Germans never knocked at the door. In another little village, a woman burst into tears when Captain Mercier knocked before entering. *Oh!* she cried, *it is the first time anyone has knocked at my door for four years!* Bowing to the Boche was obligatory or you got another fine. Even the women had to bow. It got to the point when Mayors would have to be prepared to instruct their fellow citizens. Outward signs of respect had to be taught just as much to the civilians in the poor invaded country as to the German soldier. You could not pretend not to know an officers' rank since this was taught officially.

In addition to this, schools had been closed for a long time. Not that the school teacher or school mistress had left. No, this was one of mighty Germany's diabolical schemes. It was yet another way to demoralise the French, like the newspaper *La Gazette des Ardennes*[19] and all their dealings with civilians. Yes, it was striking at Bulson, Authes, Chaumont, and in all these villages I established with certainty for my own benefit that the Boche had closed or rather requisitioned the school. Two years ago, three years ago, at any moment in the war, military authorities had needed the school premises for some unknown reason. This occurred even 60 kilometres behind the lines, in any small village where there appeared to be troops. But what about the school teacher, I would ask naively, perhaps there wasn't one anymore? Of course there was, they always replied. Miss So-and-so, old Mr So-and-so were still there.

The Boche were like Satan. What tortuous methods they used to undermine our future! They had conceived the idea that leaving our children uneducated could do us harm. They would certainly have extended this method to the big cities, and may well have done so by the way – something I don't know. But the Germans always behaved in their own best interest, and knew there would be a universal outcry if they acted openly against State education by closing classes in big centres.

Civilians were the slaves of this fearful machine, the German army. There was no freedom, no property any more. Gradually, the Germans held everything to ransom. Cattle, farm machinery, land, all means of culture were soon in their hands. They exploited our country for themselves and employed the labour force without pay, or paid them a miserable salary which they easily funded by the many fines they inflicted for the smallest breach of their innumerable rules. The Germans wanted everything. Even women had to work. Their iron law forced everyone, men and women, old and young, to work for a set number of hours each day. No one was exempt. And what terrible work it was, this organised labour of our poor enslaved country! In the country people were guarded by soldiers. All of them, woodcutters, farm workers were assembled like prisoners and went to their worksites with their guards.

Town-dwellers were often deported to the country and young girls from the towns employed on the farms, even though they were unaccustomed to this kind of work. Not a single resource was neglected, cattle as well as humans, tools and the land itself were subjected to the savage brutality and the greed of the Germans. There were no exceptions, rich and poor had to submit and give the fruits of their labour to this despicable army. Officers took local women as servants. The *Kasino* monopolised the prettiest girls to serve the *Junkers (young men)*. Cleaning the villages, sweeping the streets, keeping the officers' lodgings tidy, were the jobs of civilian men and women. In a word, there was no respite, the inhabitants were left with nothing.

In the whole of the Meuse region we never found a single cow, calf or horse. There were no dogs left either, as a tax had to be paid. The only animals that were tolerated or rather hidden in cellars and sheds, were rabbits. Every family kept a few, as many as they could, for this was the only addition to the Red Cross menu allowed by the Germans. There was no lack of vegetables but the Germans only allowed a small garden for private cultivation. I couldn't be sure if they had actually forbidden the civilians to farm. At any rate they had made this impossible by seizing animals, agricultural tools and land. The only milk people had was American condensed milk. One goat was all I saw in all the villages I went through. This goat was the only animal remaining from a farm which might have stabled forty horses, a cowshed of twenty or thirty cows, and so on. The farmer's wife told me the vet had let her keep the goat this last spring, 'because it was too old and would not be able to travel'.

In some regions the inhabitants managed to hide a few beehives in their basements, but without this precaution everything would have been requisitioned. There was no sign of hen houses or poultry. In previous years, when the inhabitants still kept some possessions, they were fined if they did not deliver their products to the *Kommandantur*. A good woman who, with difficulty, had fed her poultry, supplied her eggs (so many per hen per week) to the Germans. They allowed her to keep a few (so many per family member) for a 1.50 Marks payment per egg. Yes, the producers had to buy their own produce! Each beehive had to produce so many pounds of honey, although the Germans seemed to have turned a blind eye to any surplus from the hives. There had, indeed, been a surplus, for this is how I ate honey in a few villages: illicit honey 'stolen' at the risk of a fine to the all-powerful German.

Furniture, household stuff and all those little things that made up family life, were destroyed systematically by the Germans, with the thought as they burnt and plundered or even ravaged our homes, that they were undermining yet more the vitality of France. It is to this systematic destruction that we owe the strategic burning of villages, the exiles, the deportations. Burning went on till the end. Verrières was an example, destroyed on November 6th in spite of President Wilson's warnings. For weeks all the inhabitants of the Ardennes had been encouraged to evacuate their villages. This would have enabled the Germans to remove what remained of furniture and bedding. Every day the inhabitants saw the convoys of old cupboards, mattresses, furniture taken from the villages near the front, and they did not forget the lesson. They obstinately ignored the entreaties of the 'kind' Germans who claimed they were saving them from the Allied shells. In the last months of the war, ever since they knew their days were numbered, the Germans not only withdrew their large guns, their heavy equipment – a sign that the French interpreted as a good omen – but they still put pressure on the villagers for the little that remained. Each unit as it passed requisitioned a certain number of beds, mattresses, sheets, eiderdowns and so on and naturally they took them all away. When the next unit complained bitterly about their poor reception and not being able to rest comfortably, it happened all over again and the mayor had to make use once more of all his stratagems: one person provided the bed, someone else the mattress, a third one the blankets. When we arrived, all that remained for a family of two or three was one or two complete beds at the most. The rest had been plundered.

The poor women inhabitants would explain how the last German officer had taken away the pair of sheets and the blanket, or they would get out of a hiding place an eiderdown or a pillow which had been stored there and protected from German greed. At Authes, the mayor's wife took all the copper parts of the stove out of a hole in the garden, because the Boche had requisitioned everything. String, copper, linen, blankets. This good old woman, the mayor's wife, told us she had once burnt all the string in the house so as not to give it to the Kommandantur. Disobedience was very costly: there were fines and more severe punishments, including imprisonment. She also showed me the rough cast iron pump which had replaced the copper one. All the details cropped up in the conversation. These people did not know where to start, where to finish, they had so much to tell. They had been used to this evil for four years: waiting on the Germans, working for them, owing them everything they had, being subjected to all their outrageous impositions, all their punishments.

Not only did the Germans act, they also spoke. They spoke in the Gazette des Ardennes, as everyone knows. As I said before, they gave orders and demanded respect. They would march our people to work like slaves and considered this their due. Not complying with their regulations, not working for them was breaking German law. These brutal soldiers were able to punish: they had the means to punish because everywhere they were the masters. If one of the women in the camps refused to take on certain tasks she would face the threat of being locked up in a small cell, on bread and water, maybe for several days, or sent to Germany in exile. Those punishments were mostly for women: a good woman from St Quentin told me how she had refused to wash flea-ridden clothes and stood up to the German officer, to the terror of the other women present, and had been locked in the cell.

116

The Germans were masters of our people as if we were human cattle. They were feared so much that their demands became more and more pitiless and met with little resistance. They had no heart, and their minds were closed to all causes but their own. Because they were good soldiers, they executed orders from above and carried out tasks to the last detail. Their terrible oppression was cleverly organised to browbeat, crush and annihilate our race, destroy our wealth and deprive us of the means to rise again, whilst they took to Germany everything they could lay their hands on.

For four years the Germans were busy plundering our land. Nothing was left. Here is an example to show how much our peasants had lost. On November 10th, a youngish woman from Noyer came to take refuge with our troops in Chaumont. She cried as she was telling us that she was alone and the Germans had taken everything from her. Her house had been burnt down in 1914. All her cattle, her farm machinery had been confiscated. Her husband was dead. All she had left were two sons whom the Germans took with them.

Houses were empty, barns were empty. German requisitions had stripped the homes of everything they contained. Much worse, the land was left fallow, woods had been cut down. The Germans had removed factory machinery. Our poor forests had been devastated as the Germans cut through the undergrowth, removed full-grown trees and massacred young ones in their search for timber. Our local woods had become impenetrable and would have to be cut down in order to regrow. As my readers may have already surmised, none of this had anything to do with the rules of warfare. There was a more sinister intention behind this requisition of labour, enslavement of people, confiscation of everything French. It was for a purpose beyond the mere winning of the war.

Considering all these examples of vandalism, savagery, greed, physical and moral bondage of the French – both men and women – one becomes vaguely aware of Germany's huge plan. Somewhere at the top of the hierarchy there existed an evil intelligence. This formidable war machine was not meant only to break the front. It was an extraordinarily complex structure, which I have only partially described. If I could have got the victims to talk, these pages could be more convincing, but I have not gone so far as to try to upset my readers. I have simply told the facts and what I wrote were recollections jotted down on paper: these cannot be refuted.

The German plan was not just to beat us in battle. Greed, capturing everything, subjugating civilians, turning our population into an army of workers and using them without the slightest sympathy or pity – behind all this was another notion from which they received their strength: crushing, destroying France in all her forms, making her unable to recover.

This is why children did not go to school, civilians gave everything to Germans, labour and possessions, men were deported, young girls taken away from their families, women cooped up like prisoners. This was meant to tear French families apart. All atrocities were authorised by this ruthless plan. Destroying our monuments was another way of destroying France. Our forests annihilated, our fields left fallow, our farmers without machinery or animals: yet another way to impoverish and starve France. Our villages burned under the pretext of military strategy, our bridges blown up, our roads broken up by mines, this was sheer vandalism. France would find it hard to recover.

CHAPTER 8

My Arrival in Chaumont

FOR MY PART the war ended well. After those difficult days in Landres and on the ridge of Chatillon when the enemy had persistently held out against our bloody, ineffectual attacks, their eventual rout after our overwhelming advance on November 1st came like a ray of sunshine. I want to try and retain the memory of these last days, for no matter how joyful or unhappy, they would always remain burnt in my memory. What a relief it was after those long, depressing hours of inaction waiting in the Chatillon sector! I will always remember that I spent most of the time there at the edge of the wood we used as a command post, lazily stretched out in the sun, picking and savouring the odd broad bean and enjoying the warm rays of that autumn of 1918. On the surface, I was at peace with myself, but deep down what heavy feelings, what tragic images passed through my mind! Hope seemed crushed beneath a leaden cloak. The Germans stood their ground and our attacks on them were thwarted. When would this war finish? Would it ever finish?

In the little wood, which the Germans had spared in order to conceal their camp, the sun intensified the wonderfully rich colours of the autumn leaves. In spite of their damaged branches the trees had mostly been spared. But the war was all around us, in the air, with the bluebottles and the whiffs of mustard gas, hardly perceptible to the uninitiated. Then there was the continual threat of enemy aircraft which kept returning amidst black or white smoke from the bursts of exploding shells. On the ground, some of the debris from the last battle remained: an ammunition belt, cartridges, helmets, a few fragments of clothing, rifles, some bandages in a ditch and branches or tree trunks felled by the shelling. Here and there were graves marked by helmets, German or American, and everywhere the burrows made by the infantrymen, and trenches half filled with water – so many reminders of the hateful presence of

119

war. Despite the warm sun and the beautiful autumn, one's soul was over-whelmed by sorrow at this carnage and suffering with no end in sight.

Four days later, we were advancing with the enemy in retreat. It was the rout of the German army, after our November 1st attack which had broken their front between the Aisne and the Meuse. Every day the regiment set up camp without supplies; starving, as I mentioned earlier. On November 9th we arrived close to the Meuse, south of Sedan, and found the enemy had not held the river bank that we were soon to reach. That same day the Colonel fell ill, exhausted, and Major Anderson took command of the regiment. On the night of the 8th the front line had stopped along a ridge intersected by gullies and dominated by the little village of Chaumont – at least such was the report from the captain commanding the leading battalion. The command post of the regiment had just settled down in Bulson after marching the best part of the night. We realised that the next day we would be advancing again, because we were too far from the line and not having any information we were unable to give orders and coordinate the action of all three battalions. So we decided to move our command post forward to Chaumont, setting off about 6a.m. after a night without sleep or supplies.

The land, although indented by deep ravines, was not really mountainous. The slopes were quite steep, the valleys deep and narrow, but all these undulations were on a human scale. The woods shimmered, joyful, in the first rays of the sun, and the coming day promised to be clear and mild. Not a sound, not a shot from a rifle nor a gun; the countryside seemed peaceful, eerily quiet and deserted. This day however, like previous ones, would see the same sight of death and injury, the same bloody battle, and many brave men would 'head towards the setting sun', as the Yankee soldiers would say.

In order to reach Chaumont sooner, where we had decided to strike camp, I crossed a ravine by a scarcely visible track which left the road. On the edge of the crest, above the steep slope, a slate roof came into sight. Was this the village or some isolated houses? We climbed to the top, Major Anderson and I, and all the officers and the liaison men who formed the command post. I hurried towards the village. That first, deceptive image of a house turned out to be a covered watering-trough. But we were very close to the village, which suddenly appeared at a bend in the path between hedges of hazel trees. A pretty little village, typical of the Ardennes, perched right on the edge of the plateau, with its regular slate-covered roofs and well-built, sizeable houses, it spoke of former, more prosperous times before the war. Good fertile land and the people of Ardennes we were about to rediscover.

Everything seemed dead in the village. The street was deserted and the houses on each side seemed lifeless. Suddenly there was a cry. I was at the head of our little procession, which had scattered as we were climbing up. One cry, and all of a sudden the doors opened. As in a dream, the road was soon filled with people of all ages, women, young girls, men old and young, raising their arms to the sky, standing motionless, dumbfounded, in the middle of the street. Then the cries of joy, cries of "They are here!" becoming more ecstatic. As we approached they ran out to meet us, a woman carrying a bouquet. Our hearts too were beating fast and we quickened our pace, but even in these circumstances we had to maintain the dignity befitting our rank! And then we were surrounded, pulled to left and right, clasped in many arms and embraced. Of course I was the most fêted, being the only Frenchman. Someone presented me with a colourful bouquet of chrysanthemums. And so we made our triumphal entry into Chaumont, among these men, women and children who overwhelmed me with questions, and not knowing how best to express their joy, each one begging me to stay at their house.

Clearly we were the first to enter the village, and so I asked the people around me. "Yes", they said, "you are certainly the first, the Germans have gone, the last of them left last night". Although the villagers had seen the khaki uniforms on the nearby hill, not a single American patrol had entered the village. "You are the first!". Meanwhile the news of our arrival and the liberation spread through the village like wildfire, and quickly drew everyone onto the street. So, in this whirlwind of madness and enthusiasm which overcame everyone, amidst the tears of joy and endless shows of gratitude from the frenzied crowd, we quickly started to explore our newly conquered territory. Not only did I have to answer all the questions showered upon me, but at the same time choose our headquarters and our first-aid post, while a triumphal procession trailed behind me.

I decided to set up the headquarters in the former *Kommandantur*, a large, empty building with huge rooms, which had once been the town hall. A few women had already arrived, and I soon found out that they were clearing out the large amounts of rubbish that the Germans had left behind everywhere. One young man in particular was toiling away like somebody possessed. Scattered all over the place among the debris were grenades, which I wanted to remove as soon as possible, before there was an accident, but I was not allowed to do that, as a young girl spared me the trouble. Poor people! How happy they were to see us again! Soon the headquarters was set up in the vast premises. Our men arrived. The mayor, whom I had asked to come, approached me and straight away we had to set about locating our regiment of which we had lost all trace, and work commenced.

Our arrival had freed these good people, but they were not completely out of danger. The Boche had promised there would be a safety period of 24 hours everywhere after they had left and during their rapid retreat. Their artillery had neither the time nor the means to deploy the guns, or to fire off many shells. They had promised to spare the villages but in fact, whenever things became a little grim for them or whenever it was possible, they fired their artillery. In Chaumont, with all these civilians packed in the houses, some from the area, others evacuated from the North, I was worried at the thought of a bombardment. The first few hours were peaceful; our infantry had soon bypassed the village without even being given the order to attack, and the German machine-guns only began their 'tac-tac' when they were some 800m from the village.

As for me, now that everything was going ahead and our patrols had gone out to liaise with the battalions, I had nothing more to do. I felt the best way to use this leisure time would be to wash my face and have a shave. In war one must grab these moments when they occur. The villagers had of their own accord joined together to cook some potatoes for us, so that we could eat. Everybody was warned to be on their guard, ready to go down into the cellars for shelter at a moment's notice. So I went with a clear conscience to the nearest house and asked for some water to shave with. Those kind people were a 50-year-old villager and his wife, both honest and generous by nature. The Germans had rounded up their younger son, but the elder one, who was declared unfit for service, was actually the keen young worker who had cleaned our headquarters from attic to cellar. There were two young girls; the younger was bed-ridden and sickly, but kept smiling in spite of her illness when she saw our soldiers. The other was lively and alert, a true likeness of her mother, but aged by war and worry. Their father was happy to speak to me, and to have me in his house. How enthusiastic he was about France! He kept referring to his son, who had spent four years eaten away by not having been called up, and spoke every day of his deep regret that he was unable to serve his country. People everywhere were stunned by this sudden liberation, after going through so many emotions for so long. Undoubtedly country people are more sensitive than city-dwellers, and in this family all but the father and mother, who were more resilient, were overwhelmed by our arrival. The mother was hastily preparing an enormous dish of potatoes for our soldiers. It was indeed this family who had had the idea of organising the potato collection in the village so as to feed us. I went upstairs to the most beautiful room in the house to shave, and was shown souvenirs of 1914, fragments of shells, which had damaged cupboards and broken windows. Then I started washing.

What was so curious about the war was that I found myself living so completely in the present moment and did not worry about anything else that was happening, even if it took place only a few hundred metres away. My duty finished, and everything going to plan, there was I in the act of shaving, while our troops advanced or at least attempted to. A hail of machine-gun bullets whistled through the air and came crashing against the walls. Below me, things were turning nasty and the main road in the village had become extremely dangerous, as I soon realised from the many hissing sounds made by the bullets when they chipped little stone fragments off the walls of the headquarters that stood at the bend in the road – but I still had to shave! Even as I saw our troops advancing cautiously along a sunken, narrow path, I was amazed at myself for being able to indulge in something as frivolous as shaving, at such a solemn moment.

I went downstairs, to find our soldiers cooking potatoes and drinking coffee. I chatted for a few moments with the owner of the house and then returned to my headquarters. Nothing new there, except that all the battalions now knew we were in contact and were supporting them. A lovely cup of coffee was ready for me, flowers on the table, and a roaring fire in the stove to warm the air, already chilly on those wet November days. A number of the village women were there, handing out chocolate and coffee. What care they took of us! It seemed those people had no idea of danger, or rather no fear of danger. Some children appeared in the street whenever there was a lull in the machine-gun fire. These poor little children, mostly from the North, found all this noise new to them. Some of them had never seen the French before but had so often been told about them by their mothers. So much for my warnings!

Again I went to talk to the mayor, who had already begged me to go and have a cup of coffee with him. These people all loved their coffee. Was this the stimulus needed to revive their undernourished, exhausted and debilitated bodies; to improve their morale when they were down-hearted? This mayor was not the real mayor – he had left long ago – but an old man who had bravely taken overall responsibility on behalf of the villagers during the German requisitions, and later for the distribution of American food to the inhabitants. From the start he had taken on the thankless task of dealing with the German aggression. I insisted that all the villagers should stay at home and the old man set off again to go round the village. Eventually I was successful in that my orders were obeyed and the streets became deserted, instead of being packed with excited people feverishly bustling about and delirious with joy. I had been right to be watchful. The Boche, exasperated by our attacks and the continuing push of our infantry supported by our 37mm guns and machine-guns, started to fire huge shells at the village – the shells of their retreat, which came from a long way away, almost certainly the north bank of the river.

My heart was heavy, feeling for our poor civilians under that bombardment. These 150mm shells could have penetrated as far as the cellar floors. Luckily, no one had been hit, apart from one woman who was slightly wounded. When I went round after they were dropped (not many, fortunately), people called me over to show me the damage. In the house of a family from Roubaix, a shell had struck the chimney. It was one of the first and there was nobody yet in the cellar, but it took the masonry down the center of the chimney and smothered the fire in the hearth. Fortunately the shell had only demolished the chimney, exploding in the loft on a pile of hay. Elsewhere, people showed me their cellar which they said had withstood one of these shells. I said nothing but my eyes, which were accustomed to these things, soon noticed the cracked vault and half-loosened stones which would pose a danger to those in the cellar, even after the slightest shock from another shell. But these people were not afraid anymore: afraid of what? What mattered to them was their freedom and they had got their France back.

At the command post during the shelling, a little boy from the North had kept us company. Not a flicker of emotion crossed his bright, beautiful face when the heavy shells came crashing down, raising clouds of dust, stone and tiles. When the shelling was over, I found someone to take him home to his mother. We of the headquarters would never go down to the cellar: we had become used to bombardments and we were blasé, perhaps a good attitude for fighters. But it broke my heart to think that this child could be struck, along with us. An innocent little lad, a victim like so many others: the Boche seemed to enjoy the innumerable casualties.

At St Mihiel, we had killed a few civilians in the village, an old lady for example, but I doubt if we could have avoided it. The Boche, on the other hand, once it was clear that we were not attacking anymore, not only flattened what they had left standing of the villages we had recaptured; not only did they destroy with incendiary shells the magnificent old castle of St Benoît, a superb 18th century building, after burning and looting the church before leaving; but on top of that, they would drop more shells behind our lines, killing many, many, innocent civilians. It was the same in the Ardennes: this was all part of their campaign for the annihilation of France.

Appendix 1

MacArthur in France in 1918

WHEN THE RAINBOW Division landed in France at the end of 1917, the third to do so, it was a big unit consisting of two brigades with infantry regiments (four in all), each with three battalions of four companies, etc. – the type of division which Joffre had recommended on his military mission to the United States after the Americans had entered the war. It was a colossal unit, equivalent in numbers to two French divisions. With General Menoher as commander, its chief of staff was the already outstanding and charismatic MacArthur. It had received from the French a large task force and the backup of a commander at the division's headquarters, as well as a contingent of various sorts of officers: infantrymen, artillery, machine gunners, English-speaking captains or lieutenants, not to mention interpreters. It was when he was chief of staff of this large body (some 37,000 men) that I first saw MacArthur.

There began a period of training in trench warfare on the peaceful Langres plateau during the winter of 1917-18, followed by experience of trench warfare in Lorraine, which fortunately proved relatively quiet. MacArthur was already proving himself to be a formidable military leader, both by taking part in and observing a battalion surprise attack. The Rainbow Division played the modest role first assigned to it by the French command for inexperienced units. It participated in the last German offensive, on 14th July 1918, flanked at intervals by the French and split up into battalions, some of which fought on the front line, thus helping to stem what was to be the last German attack. Viewed, as a result, in a more favourable light, the regrouped division took part several days later in the Mangin Army[20] counter-offensive on the Château Thierry salient as far as the Ourcq. It was the beautiful summer of 1918. Again divided into battalions, the Rainbow Division, which had just played a worthy but small part in this victorious defensive campaign, embarked on the Allied armies' first victorious offensive – Mangin's offensive. From Château Thierry, which had been recaptured by the French, the Division reached the left bank of the Ourcq, right up to Villers-sur-Fère by the end of July. It was in this village, where the 165th Regiment had been brought to a three-day halt, that an incident took place, in which MacArthur seemed to be a figure of heroic fiction. Three days without moving forward, yet this Regiment, without any artillery back-up (because of blocked roads, etc.) had gained a footing on the right bank of the Ourcq, despite sustaining devastating losses – some 200 dead, who today lie buried on that very bank of the Ourcq at Seringes et Nesles. We were rocked by exhaustion, when on one fine morning in late July, MacArthur appeared in the wash house at Villers-sur-Fère which we used as our headquarters, to inform his friend McCoy, commander of the 165th, that the Germans were retreating. McCoy was crestfallen! MacArthur had been promoted to brigadier on 4 July. His friend from West Point had therefore remarked, not without a hint of jealousy on hearing of this promotion from Chaumont, 'Douglas has much charm'! [in English in the author's manuscript]. McCoy, however, was to receive his own promotion to the same rank a few days later.

On 12th September, the Rainbow Division attacked St Mihiel, flanked by French Divisions. At that time, it was not yet known that the German army was on the point of breaking up. Without any doubt the salient would have been evacuated a few days later, but we were not aware that only Austrian and Polish troops were left in front of us, nor that re-conquering the salient would be relatively easy on that morning of torrential rain, with thousands of prisoners taken.

MacArthur, with his advanced forces, started the attack from a line marked out by a long white ribbon placed in front of a network of abandoned trenches, ahead of Florey. MacArthur was, as always, that now familiar figure, wearing his flat American officer's cap, and armed with his switch.

The next stage for the Rainbow Division was the Argonne offensive, a turning point when the American army, fighting this time as a whole unit, was at a standstill. A slow advance, with frequent setbacks, and costly, but MacArthur appears again: in my eyes, a slim, elegant figure, although a Brigadier General, leading a battalion's manoeuvres to capture one of those many fortified concrete bases which the Germans had established behind their lines (the Siegfried or Kriemhilde Stellung).

All that remained was the occupation of the Rhine at Remagen, from winter 1918 to spring 1919. There I saw MacArthur again, as a guest of Caldwell, his colleague of the 83th Brigade, who, according to MacArthur, had made only two good things: his two daughters. Scathing at times, but this was an aspect of MacArthur's character.

MacArthur ranked among the élite of American officers. One of them, Lieutenant Colonel Donovan, later Colonel of the 165th, said when describing to a French officer the first bombardment that he experienced in the Forest of Parroy: "C'est un bon excitement!" MacArthur had the simplicity and charm of unfailing courage, elegance in his demeanour (which was also an attribute of his less fortunate friend McCoy, who died young), and most of all, the potential of a captain such as Alexander [the Great]. Many of us would not forget, during a later conflict, that it was on French soil that MacArthur, together with the Rainbow Division, had his first, terrible training in warfare.

A. Rérat, 1974

Appendix 2

Crossing of the Ourcq by the
165th American Regiment
at the end of July 1918

I WROTE THIS ACCOUNT a few months after the events, when I was starting as a teacher at the Lycee of Nancy. I had gained the qualification known as the Agrégation of the Demobilised[21] in October 1919. This was before my marriage, and I was living at Mme Pignan's, Rue du Vieil Aitre.

The 165th Regiment was made up of Irish American Catholics, hence the presence and the importance of Father Duffy. All these Irishmen from New York were volunteers, but their numbers were enlarged by an assortment of reinforcements. The 165th Regiment, like a French regiment, was made up of three battalions. Each battalion had four companies as opposed to the three in a French regiment. The companies had a strength of about 250 men, not the 150 or fewer in a French company. Joffre had been to the United States in 1915 and had advocated this form of organisation, which meant a reduction in the requirement for officers. The companies were identified by a letter; those of the third battalion were designated I, K, L, M; the capital J had been omitted, perhaps to avoid confusion.

I was appointed to the 3rd Battalion, 165th Regiment, in December 1917 as an instructor. Then as things went on, the number of instructor officers per regiment was reduced from three to one. I stayed on, but as 'liaison' officer, a new title meant to spare the feelings of the Americans. Captain Mercier, who was with Major Donovan (1st Battalion), became responsible for liaison with Brigade (165th and 166th Regiments).

The Ourcq episode (July-August 1918) was at a turning point of the First World War. On July14th, 1918, the last attack of the Germans under Lüdendorff had broken down (action at Auberive for my battalion). The account by Father

Duffy in '*Father Duffy's Story*' (published in 1919), was quoted in my book '*In The English Boat*' (1934), when I used the name of Roy instead of my real name of Rérat.

Until then the troops of the 42nd (Rainbow) Division had operated only as so many separate battalions, not even as regiments. The pursuit of the German army by the French army to Chateau Thierry, then on towards the Ourcq, launched on the heels of the almost total defeat of the German offensive of 14th July, thus marked the turning point of the war, since the allied offensives did not cease until the armistice of 11th November. I must observe, in passing, that the sudden change from defensive to offensive on the part of the allies was due to the arrival in France of one and a half million Americans.

The names of Donovan, Anderson (2nd Battalion), McKenna (3rd Battalion), are those of the commanders of these battalions on the Ourcq. The Colonel was still the delightful McCoy, a friend at West Point of MacArthur, the latter had been promoted on 4th July 1918 (Independence Day) from colonel, chief of staff of the Rainbow Division, to brigadier, commanding of one of the two brigades of the Division. McCoy would be promoted brigadier a little while later, and never ceased to be extremely friendly to me. For example, when he had returned to America he wrote a letter to the American army, in order that I might receive the Distinguished Service Cross, which had already been awarded but the medal had never been sent to me. McCoy died young, in about 1925, after having played an active role in the Philippines and in Japan.

People of the French Mission are also mentioned in my account, for example Jacobson, an artilleryman and artillery liaison officer with the 42nd Infantry Division: a lovely man who never spared his efforts, witness our meetings both in Villers-sur-Fere and Mareuil.

In retrospect, my 1919 judgment of the Americans is much too severe. Their army was in its infancy and the Division did not operate as a Division until the Ourcq battle, hence the mistakes and the weaknesses. Neither officers nor men had learned through long and bitter experience to maintain cohesion as a unit throughout. Hence this climate of 'do what you like' and lack of liaison, exemplified by Commander Donovan going his own way and having a stroll with his men around the front line.

Rérat, 1974

Footnotes

1 Vicker-Berthier light machine-gun based on a French design.

2 Alan Seegar, American poet (1888-1916) fought and died in WW1, serving with the French Foreign Legion so that he could fight for the Allies. The US did not enter the war until 1917.) His poem *I have a Rendezvous with Death* is very well known.

3 Known later as 'The Second Battle of the Marne'.

4 General Gouraud, 1867-1946, Commander of the French Fourth Army in WW1, gained distinction for his use of elastic defence during the Second Battle of the Marne.

5 The author had been called up in 1914 and fought in the French army until 1917, when he became an instructor attached to the 42nd Division, US Army.

6 The Stokes 3-inch trench mortar; fired a mortar bomb of 11 pounds to a range of between 100 and 800 yards.

7 The author notes: "In my company in the French 230th Infantry Regiment, both types of officers were represented. The company commander excelled by his gallantry, slightly exaggerated and theatrical: for example he would get his revolver out against alleged fugitives and even obtained a mention for an incident of this nature. The other type was Lapierre, common sense personified. The former would not have hesitated to risk his men's lives almost needlessly, on impulse, against the enemy. The latter would only have risked lives advisedly and was an example of boundless dedication, always efficient, and quietly so. Unfortunately the former was the preferred type in the army, where bluster has its share of importance."

8 In 1917 the Headquarters of the American Expeditionary Force was located in Chaumont, Haute Marne.

9 After the defeat of France in the Franco-Prussian War, Alsace and a part of Lorraine were annexed by the Germans. French was not taught in schools anymore.

10 Pierre-Simon, Marquis de Laplace, (born 23 March 1749, Beaumount-en-Auge, Normandy, France; died 5 March 1827, Paris). French mathematician, astronomer, and physicist who is best known for his investigations into the stability of the solar system.

11 'Classe 16' refers to the year of conscription into the army. This young man was born in 1896 and was called up in 1916, at age 20; the age of mobilisation for most men in the place where he lived.

[12] The author notes: "Later, Haugh would be made Governor of Ohio – it was all engineered for him."

[13] On this narrow road, the only road to Verdun from Bar-le-Duc, 6000 lorries would transport reinforcements, material and munitions to the battle of Verdun (1916) every day. Hence the name 'Voie Sacrée' (Sacred Way).

[14] This was very likely to have been the Spanish flu, which led to the Influenza Pendemic (January 1918 to December 1920).

[15] 'Le brave des braves', a nickname earned by Maréchal Ney (1769-1815), Marshal in Napoléon Bonaparte's 'Grande Armée'.

[16] A house in military slang.

[17] The nickname given to Avallet, the author's orderly.

[18] Possibly refers to the French occupation of the Rhineland in 1919. The French Eighth Army and Tenth Army originally constituted the French forces involved in the occupation. On 21 October 1919, they were combined to form the French Army of the Rhine, stationing between 25,000 and 40,000 French colonial soldiers in the region. Racist anxieties concerning the presence of Black soldiers in the French occupation army led to allegations of mistreatment of the German civilian population, resulting in a widespread campaign by the German right-wing press. However, General Henry Truman Allen reported to the US Secretary of State that "the wholesale atrocities ... are false and intended as political propaganda".

[19] For countries participating in the First World War the press was the principal means of controlling public opinion. Newspapers were subject to strict censorship and were obliged to publish official communiqués. In the occupied territories the Germans controlled the flow of news, publishing the paper *La Gazette des Ardennes* in November 1914 (printed in Charleville-Mézières). Distributed by the Kommandanturen, it was originally a weekly publication with a small circulation (c.4,000 copies) whose sole purpose was to publish translations of official German communiqués. Conscious of the hostility towards *La Gazette des Ardennes* the German Army attempted to solve the problem by publishing the names of the French soldiers taken prisoner or who died in the prison camps (in all, more than 250,000 names would be published) and by October 1917 they were printing 175,000 copies of every edition. The last edition was issued on 2 November 1918.

[20] General Charles Mangin (1866-1925) epitomised the 'offensive spirit' mandated by the French Army high command prior to the start of war in August 1914, by figures such as Joffre and Lanrezac. Mangin's out-and-out aggression did not always pay dividends. Despite renowned victories, at first Charleroi and then Verdun, his

reputation plummeted following the disastrous Nivelle Offensive during April and May 1917. Mangin's Sixth Army bore the brunt of the main attack during Second Aisne, the centrepiece of Robert Nivelle's bold assault. With the failure of the attack Mangin was, along with Nivelle, rapidly removed from effective command (Nivelle to North Africa). Mangin suffered from being one of few senior French officers to publicly favour Nivelle's doomed strategy.

21 Agrégation: a qualification awarded after a competitive examination for acceptance as a teacher at a Lycée (State secondary school).

The Author's Original Notes

'Organization of the Ground by the Infantry Company'
and
'A Few Lesons in Tactics to be given to NCOs and Younger Officers'

ORGANIZATION OF THE GROUND BY THE INFANTRY COMPANY.
Notes written after the Baccarat Sector.

We have been up to now in a so-called quite sector. This means we have found all of the defensive works organized whether in open warfare or in position warfare, we will have to face from now on the big problem of holding ground effectively, under fire, and a ground without woods, trenches, dugouts or boyaux, the line of defence being made up of a few separate trench elements. The idea to bear in mind is to transform immediately that porr system into a well conceived, well executed position-this under shell fire with limited means either men or material. Though it looks an impossible proposition, efforts belongs to every company commander to create a perfect tranchwork in a few days, I mean a first line trench deep and with traverses and wires, cts (one at least, two if possible) going to his P. C. and the support platoon, and finally the support trench itself. This can be done on a perfectly new front and under fire provided the weather is favorable and the working well planned. We must remember that a defensive trenchwork is the first step towards the offensive. A big offensive action cannot be harbored from the open ground. My division was relieved at Verdon in September 1916 and left a shell holed ground to another division whose mission was to organize trenches, C.T.S?, dugouts, etc., preparatory to the attack on Ft. Vaux which was to be the part of my division. This was perfectly executed and meant the success of our attack in October. True that one can very well live and fight in shell holes, isolated trench elements. But instead of isolated men we want co-ordinated action. A defensive trench work means a more efficient resistance, economy of men, so helps the spare divisions for real offense work elsewhere. A defensive trench work is again the only means of fighting the enemy artillery. In fact all things called defensive have an indirect offensive value// Here are a few advices which will help you to carry out your organization of the ground, yet these will not serve you at all if your officers, NCOS and men are not familiar with the necessity of trench works as soon as stabilized warfare begins. With trench works you will command your troops, support it. With trench works be able to carry in-formation to you so that you will always know, others too, how to act. Further more you contribute indirectly to the future offensives or the offensives carried out elsewhere. Proselytise the men. A soldier in a shell hole where he stays quite all day, from which he can move at night, where he can lie in ambush for the enemy and hit him by surprise more than from a trench, does not feel the need of these niceties, such as wire, a continuous firing trench, etc. Make him realize it by education him on the subject. // The first day after a battle, what is the appearance of the grounds? A few groups of men in isolated shallow holes with no specially studied distribution of automatic rifles, etc. What we must fight against is the duration of such a state of things. The carelessness natural in a battle, also the excuse of the bombardment, lack of materials, fatigue of the men are to be guarded against. The company commanders and cheif of platoons must plan as well as Field Officers With white tape sent from the office of the Colonel, they will lay out their firing trench, profiting by the dusk of the dawn to carefully inspect the grounds. They will work together, the

Captain seeing his platoon commanders successfully and discussing
on the spot itself how some particular feature of the ground is to
be looked after, study field or fire, emplacements of Automatic Rifles,
and V. B.'s. They will also draw the line of wires with the white tape.
A new position executed after this preliminary inspection will not be
ideal, but there will be some sense in it. Remember that to obtain
a good trench in effect, you must yourself outline even the traverses
(with tape or if no tape is obtained with a party of two or three men
with picks outlining them). Nothing will XXXXXXX help your wiring
parties in the dark like the white piece of tape marking their outward
limit, etc. You will have the satisfaction of shaping things out
according to your mind. This first part is the exclusive business of
the officers or the NCO'S, the next depends most on the men. Yet
the will of the Captain is all and all. One regiment will be able to
make wires, tranches, dugouts, the next under the same circumstances,
will prefer idleing; the precarious life of the shell hole. The theory
is; generally works are impossible in the day time, except in woods,
ravines, dugouts. So the men rest all day excepting for the necessary
lookouts. An average of six to eight lookouts will perfectly cover the
sector, support platoons and C. P. commanders lookouts included. There
is a big majority of men rested and ready to work. At night everybody will work a few hours. The carrying parties will be taken from
the support platoons(or company in reserve for the battalions). The
main body of the first line company will dig, and place wires. It
takes a very small number of men to watch a front of 500 or 600 yards.
All men being almost at their emplacement of combat, two men in
six can watch, for example, can watch(and rest) working a relief with
the four others. In these short summer nights everybody is up, getting
his sleep in the day. The firing trench, its wires, next its dugouts,
dumps, all these are the work of the platoons in line. If you have
wiring parties, do not put to many men to cover them. Two will
sufficiently protect a party of eight or ten, with grenades, at a
distance of thrity or forty yards in front of the wire lines. An
attack comes and all have to fall back to the trench and the regular
emplace ents. Economize your men by having only the necessary amount
of lookouts,covering detachments,etc. Ask for reasonable output of
work from each. Mounting guard will be a relaxation and change. Never
divert big parties from the first line platoons to far away emplacements
of work. But you can take a few men even from the first line platoon
at any time if need be unless these platoons are very depleted.

The support platoons will dig the CT's going to the
first line, their shelter trenches and support paralel. They carry
materials where necessary. If you have not enough engineer tools,
work by reliefs of half.

As a rule you allot to a platoon or a half platoon the
work that appeals most to them, that is, which is of most use to them.
Stimulate interest by XXXXXXXXX varying XXXXXXXXX the works. Yet
if a group of men grows keen on some particular occupation, also to
avoid the inevitable waste of time consequence on new men resuming
unfinished work, try to interest your teams by varities in the same
occupation(carrying materials for a dugout is a change to digging the
dugout, etc). The Captain is the engineer of his line of trenches.
He is not liable to receive any help from anybody except the Major.

He gets to know his ground so well that he only **is** chiefly competent, also his chief of platoons. Though his plan must fit in the more general one shaped out by the Colonel and he complies with orders on this subject, yet he never waits for orders to start.

Here are a few practical recipes on trench digging; have your men by teams of two(general one pick, one shovel), Give them their task(so much deep, so much in length), Control the results according to hard or soft ground, etc., and let them go back to rest as soon as it is over. This is better than exacting hours of work. Ask rather for an amount of work.

Have good solid traverses (three steps square or about). The width will be good at the start, if not your trench will be to narrow at the bottom(one meter or one meter 20 cm. is a fitting start). Whenever you leave off working,camouflage. The thing to be done preliminary to camouflaging is flattening out the XXXXXX parapits which the men cannot help making at the outset for prtection(which is rather to be encouraged provided you correct it). One **inch** is the maximun height for the parapet or parados. Avoid making heaps which give away your trench or dugout. Leave a [   ] each side(one foot wide). The means of camouflaging is grass, foliage, etc. The officer chief of platoon is present whenever there is more than one half of the platoon at work. Make it a rule. Let the officers show by a keen contraol what interest they take in the work, which conveys to the men an idea of the importance of the work. The captain mathimatically makes out what length of trench must be carried out according to soil, etc. Let the officers and the NCO's in charge have sticks measuring one meter. The captain also must deside and choose the working hours according to shell fire, lightx (dusk,moonlight,etc.)

WIRES: The white tape will help very much. Also triangle made with sticks or moved along the tape, allowing to place the rods accurately in the darkest of nights. Remember that wires will rarely be placed at the proper distance from the trench(forty meters at the outside). Generally in a fight they are placed close to the trench. Correct that,for these can help, they will always be destroyed by artillery registering on the trench, while wires camouflage far from the trench, even in small quanity, will be always overlooked by the enemy and stop him.

Preparation of materials(coils of barb wire chiefly) is necessary(these coilsare 20 to 25 meters long). Men cannot handle a XXXXXXX big heavy roal of Iroquois wires. This is done in the day time even by the first line people.

SANDBAGS: Not to be used much except for reparing broken down trenches, cheifly for Automatic rifle posts and the entrance of dugouts(more resisting power than mere earth).

DUGOUTS: UseX narrow and deep slit trenches placed in the zones spared by xxtillxxx shelling, and well camouflaged(covered with branches, sheet iron, with a layer of earth, canvas peices with a thin layer of dust and grass, etc. Start dugouts as soon as you get materials, beginning by the company P. C. and the support platoons. There you will get the help of the pioneers whom the Major will send to you for that purpose.

Start your dugouts well. That is place the first wooden frame at leat two inches from the surface of the virgin ground. The entrance is always the weak point in a dugout(the germans generally reinforce it with concrete). If some troop is hereby you can always find materials with which to start dugout. Send your carpenters with saw and hatchets to prepare frames in day time, etc. A captain must develope in his company all kinds of specialists. he must know his men according to their abilities. One is wonderful and rapidly preparing grenadier posts. Another is a good carpenter, another is unable to handle a pick and has to be use as a lookout, etc. Let the company commander start a kind of a group of pioneers in his own bunch of men. The Liaison agents anyway always help the pioneers at the captains dugout, etc. Use every one.

You will never insist to much on camouflage. Camouflage begins with a good thorough policing(as tin boxes, arms on parapets giving away the different G. C.'s), with a trench the parapets of which are flattened out, etc. The rest is a matter of ingenuity(grass,sticks, layers of mold on the top surface) on the whole appeal to the common sense of your men for every new effort you ask. As it is always for the general good, your cause is always easyto defend. Mention casually to your men as they work, why and wherefore of a connecting trench, etc, the specific reason explaining each particular case. Then you will find a good will that it is impossible to exhaust. Every new output means a saved life for you, for the next people generally. Yet even you will profit by your efforts. These remarks are far from being exhaustive, but they give a general line for a start.

TRENCH LIFE.

Being a commander of troops at all stages is cheifly a matter of foresight and method. Here are a few examples falling under this head.

RELIEF: Always work it out with as complete and accurate details as possible, simplicity being though the necessary limitation.

Replacements for Guides: Time for these guides: Order of the platoons(definite reasons accounting for it). Take the NCO's into the secret of every detail.

Before you take a sector give as much dope as you can. You reconnoiter generally 24 hours in advance and you will see your company for a few hours before taking over the sector. This is the time to assemble your whole company, tell them your impression, what kind of a life and of efforts will be asked from every one, etc. Impart all the wisdom you have at all times. Remember that beside the plan of defense you are supposed to get a plan of work, also all the details as to the enemy habits of shelling, infantry activity. Finally you must know all about supplies, time, ways of the preceding unit, where water is to be obtained. All this can be left in writing even on the worst front. Do it yourself for the next man. This plan of work will help you at the start, while you are still unacquainted with the terraine. Follow it as closely as possible unless there are gross mistakes in it. This is not time for discussing tastes or niceties. But for a continuous action. Stick to the existing plan, when it has received some beginnings of an execution. It is altogether better than a brand new one which agrees more with your ideas and is more pleasant to you because it is yours. Spare your men mistakes.

Spare your men mistakes in the route and better loss of time by
carefully thinking over the relief and get all knowledge you can
out of the chief of the preceeding unit so as to avoid his mistakes.
    A relieving company must walk very slowly. The tail of the
column in single file(as in a boyau for example) can never follow the
beginning except by running very fast at times, even when the head
goes very slowly. Have frequent halts, word about which is passed
down. Pass the dangerous points as quickly as possible, checking
up immediately after. Guides are supposed to warn you of these points.
Never trust a guide entirely; that is, check on him all the time so that
if he gets lost you will be able to find the right way by compass. The
best for the first night is to have stand-to all night in the first
line anyhow.

    SUPPLIES: Food will be received cold and in the night. It will
probably be carried to you by parties from another battalion or company.
Each platoon commander must see that it is warmed under the shelter of
some corrugated iron, or some rigged up field range and fire. The
necessary amount of men for carrying the food of one French platoon is
four or five. The time of meeting at the P. C. of the captain, the
number of each platoon food party, all this is the matter of a special
note of the captain to the chief of the platoon. If the distribution
is at the battalion P. C. send these four groups under a NCO.

    A chief of platoon or captain attends to the question of supplies
very carefully. Even if you have to live on reserve rations let each
platoon prepare a dish of hot chocolate or Cube Bouillon Soup or coffee.
This has to be prepared anywhere. One hot drink in the course of
these cool nights, one hot soup dish early before dawn, this will make
your men last and endure these hardships. Water is necessary. The
captain will get the information on that subject at the relief? Fill
all canteens at night. Send parties with buckets if you discover a well,
fountain, riverlet. On a newly conquered ground, the water must be
first qualified good by the Doctor who must see the spot, etc. He is
the man to be called upon at all times to inquire into the question of
water and examine as soon as possible the surroundings of a water spring.
Send for him. This constant attempt of bettering living conditions, as
exemplified in this food matter will create a great and fine spirit of
friendship and devotion between officers and men. Spread this information on watering points from the first night of the relief. Water is
absolutely necessary in a hot sector. All this means cooking utensils
in the platoon, buckets or canteens with straps(like the French) for
carrying drinks. Also it means that every platoon must develop a cook,
even two cooks(one per on half platoon as with the French). Our men
prefer this man not to mount guard, dig, etc. But he washes the dishes
warms up the foods. He is honest, devoted to his section, generally
middle aged. He realizes the tremendous importance of a well fed soldier
and works for the wellfare of his people like a faithfull dog, that he
is.

    CARRYING PARTIES: Let these men have only pistols and belts
or grenades-no rifles. Check them very minutely. Remeber the
golden rule; the officer goes with the platoon when more than half of
the platoon goes. All chiefs accompany their troops whatever their
mission. Every carrying party commander has a piece of paper on which
he writes the materials carried. He reports of it at his destination
and asks for a check if the man he reports to forgets it.

The working party commander must report the number of men to the
officer who is to employ him. When you fix a task for a working
party who have traveled from far accross barrages, etc., always
think of this surplus labor, the going and coming. T.e working party
does not leave its work without having been checked by the   G.O.
A carrying party is generally sent two or three times if more materials
are announced by the major. If not, it is used on some digging.

Control is necessary at every moment. It does not mean mistrust,
but avoids misunderstanding, does away with complaints and reports. A
clear will and a clear mind of the elements of success.

NOTE: Fire from an Aeroplane is not dangerous for men in trenches,
provided niches are prepared(firing posts, grenadier posts) so as to
be protected from enfilade fire. But observation byplanes are dangerous
for it means the destruction of the trench by artillery fire if the enemy
attacks, also harrassing fire in ordinary circumstances. Groups standing in trenches are distinctly seen by planes(no so by balloons). W.en
they fly low the utmost care must be taken to hide well. A preventive
measure as usual is a thorough camouflage.

2nd NOTE: In a relief have your First Sergeant reconnoiter the
wells, the material and tool dumps. Control as soon as he takes over
the trench what ammunition of all kinds there is and in what state.

OPEN WAR FARE. General Idea: A fight does not imply that units are thrown into it indiscriminately. One word is descriptive of a completely wrong frame of mind about this war; The phrase "Feed In" is to be guarded against and proscribed. The history of the war has condemned this phrase uterly. In 1915 even as far as 1916, the French had people of the old school who were still using this metaphor; They compared war to a gigantic fire where Units, Regiments, Divisions were thrown in like so many bundles of straw, and where they were soon spent. This is a criminal idea about the war. These people of the old school, with these or similiar metaphor in their heads, have been done away with. The destruction of the enemy must not imply our own self destruction. If we accept passively the fact of our own destruction being wrought at the same time with that of the enemy, or more over we raise this fact to the level of a principle, we wrong the men at trusted to our command, we wrong ourselves. Let us this destroy this absurd theory . Let us also guard against these facts which spring from it.

ECONOMY OF MAN POWER. No.reinforcements must be sent when a failure is due to enemy machine guns, enemy superiority of artillery, to enemy entrenchments strongly held. The remedy is not number. Far from it. Hence the following rules: No chief must ask for reinforcements is such circumstances. No reinforcements can be granted, if they imply crowding or mixing up of Units in an offensive. In the defensive, all demands for reinforcements must be carefully looked into, people who ask for more men will be the same who do not utlize their men to the best. Economy of the man power is to be our constant aim; Therefore let us learn
    Not to fight Machine Gun with a thick frontal line of men.
    To manouvere the enemy by outflanking the resistance,
    which implies plenty of room, many empty spaces and
    Few men in the first line.
    Not to ask for reinforcements, but find the means with what we have
  of overcoming the enemy.
Again a defensive line is not held everywhere with a continuous row of men. Let us learn the importance of flanking fires, let us practice this as often as possible . Economize the mens lives, their pains too. Infact whenever men are sent anywhere, let us always feel sure they have a mission nobody else can cover and fulfill.

A FEW TACTICAL PROBLEMS. A few circumstances where certain definite rules can be applied are the following and they must often recur under the form of a problem and manouevres;
    1. How to cross a bare crest under artillery observation and fire. If there is no barrage, get as near as possible to the line of visibility. Take appropriate formations and cross it by surprise and quick rushes. Stop at the next cover and check up.
    II. How to cross a barrage: A barrage cannot be kept up indefinitely (It is a question of ammunition, of cooling down of the guns, etc.) Two circumstances may occur; The fire curtain of the shells is continuous or there is a gap, if there is a gap it is to be used. If not , wait for the slackening of the fire and getting close to the curtain (200 yds.are a safe margin), cross it when the fire is suspended.
    III. Never stay in the open, under observation. Never try to cross a barrage when there is no obsolute necessity and there is time for some

141

delay. No hurry, such as the golden rule of a fight.

IV. It never pays to suffer casualties, not even in order to gain time. Casualties always mean final failure. For example; There is two ways to a place, one defilated but four kilometers long. The other only one kilometer long but in plain view. Experience demonstrates that (except runners) no troops can reach the destination quicker by the latter even if it can do it without too many losses. This applies to artillery fire, but chiefly to Infantry fire. In the former case movements are still possible, chiefly with the slow observation system of the German artillery. In the latter they are totally impossible.

An axis of march is meant to avoid mixing up of units, Regiments etc. But, mixing up of Units is a temporary, probably easily to be remedy. So even for the prupose of not getting mixed up with your neighbors, do not run into casualties by following your axis of march strictly. Except when it leads you straight into a barrage a beaten road. In the end there is no case where by suffering casualties you will fulfill your mission better. When there is two ways of arriving at a result, one without casualties, the other with casualties, always prefer the former, even if an appearance the latter would afford great advantages. In other words there id no advantage to be preferred to that of safety, I mean when a given result is obtained both ways and the mission of the troops is fulfilled.

In the defensive, teach digging in, camouflage. The duty of the N.C.O is to prevent bunching. No one shell must be liable to hit two men at once, etc.

The value of the different covers must be taught with great care in open warfare: The enemy artillery has probably small scale maps, only few others, if any. Teach your N.C.O. the reading of the 80,000 scale map. The value of ravines is increased a 100 per cent if they are not shown on maps. Any details such as a sand pit, deep river course or protected embankment which is not shown on the 1/20,000 map is of very great value. Avoid small woods in a bare open space. On the reverse the value of big woods is very great and chiefly of any rpotection afforded by embankments, woods etc., as they cannot be located accurately and camouflage is perfect. The choice of covers is to be given great attention to and a lot of time devoted to this.

LIAISON: It is the keystone in any action.

In order to practice liaison with efficiency a machine gun platoon and 37 m/m gun ought to be attached to each battalion in the drill period.

Then we could practice:

Asking machine gunners for a help against a given enemy nest. (These could practice on the other hand finding appropriate emplacements((emplacements of readines for help in the majority of circumstances, choice of new emplacements according to help to be furnished))

The machine gunners and 37 m/m crew will have to tell unit they are attached to where they are, where they move, what help they can give it at all times etc. This means of course experience runners. The runners must be educated by means of the map and khexxxmstxhaxahlaxtxxnxxd oriented compass they must be able to read the map, orient it, locate on it their emplacements. Let them practice: Going from one point of the map to another, send them to a given P.C. to another where their arrival will be checked (Time, route, etc.) Let everybody be imbued with this idea: That he will be no good if his superior do not know where hh and his troop are. This again is a matter of close liaison.

The same duty applies to the Major who must tell his company commanders

his exact emplacement, etc.   This method of telling where one is applies
to stokes, machine gun, 37 m/m as well as to Infantry platoons and companies
and the Supply parties of each unit (rolling kitchens). The pioneers etc.
The first thing to be done when a new emplacement is reached, unless the
information is not wanted, is to send back word about it, if possible a
sketch too.
     I insist on the importance of a written message,etc.
     A written message is valuable because there can be no mistake in the
transmitting of the contents, because the man who writes his message will
when he re-reads himself see his inaccuraty of language.   All orders for
similar reasons must be careful written down,   No man can boast of a head
well organized enough for dictating a perfect message at once, with no mistakes, no omissions.

TEAM WORK. A good liaison will result in a good team work.
          Necessity of team work.
          I.   In each speciality of the platoon between the V.B's and(ex-
istingneed for conscentration on certain targets) between the machine guns.
          II. Between the different specialties in the platoon, Company,
and Battalion and existing between 37 m/m and Infantry between Machine gun
and Infantry, etc.
          III. Between two different units it is needful to know where the
next people are, platoons, companies, etc. ,what they intend what they
intend doing etc.
          All this must be illustrated by manoeuvre beginning by the
and progressively up to the Battalion.

A FEW RULES FOR TEACHING THESE VALUABLE IDEAS.

          Start with a plan of what you will demonstrate. Be sure
that everybody knows your meaning and understands the location.   Do
not teach everything at the same time, but be satisfied when one great
lesson is well known by both NCO's and men.
          Apply the rules to yourself: for example what has been
said about taking, sending written notes, but be constantly put into
practice. Prepare your problems on maps and put them in writing so as
to supply the failure of memory and correct the mistakes you always make
at the first blush.
          Theorise, but always illustrate your theories so as to make
them perfectly plain. Cultivate the intelligence and judgement powers
in your men, at the same time in yourself.

The map opposite shows the movement of the Headquarters, 165 US Infantry Regiment in the period 1917 to 1919.